D1524157

"Sense of Purpose in Life Linked to Lower Mortality and Cardiovascular Risk." *ScienceDaily*, December 3, 2015. Accessed June 1, 2017. www.sciencedaily.com/releases/2015/12/151203112844.htm.

Span, Paula. "Living on Purpose." The New Old Age Blog, *New York Times*, June 3, 2014. https://newoldage.blogs.nytimes.com/2014/6/03/living-on-purpose/.

Stossel, Scott. "What Makes Us Happy, Revisited." *Atlantic*, May 2013. https://www.the atlantic.com/magazine/archive/2013/05/thanks-mom/309287/.

Thomas, William H. *What Are Old People For? How Elders Will Save the World*. St. Louis: VanderWyk & Burnham, 2007.

Tillich, Paul. *The Courage to Be*. New Haven: Yale University Press, 1952.

US Government Accountability Office. "Retirement Security: Most Households Approaching Retirement Have Low Savings" (GAO-15-419), May 12, 2015. https:// www.gao.gov/products/GAO-15-419.

Vick, Karl. "The Home of the Future." *Time*, March 23, 2017. http://time.com/4710619/the-home-of-the-future/.

Waldinger, Robert. "What Makes a Good Life? Lessons from the Longest Study on Happiness." TED video. Accessed July 13, 2017. https://www.ted.com/talks/robert waldinger_what_makes_a_good_life_lessons_from_the_longest_study_on_hap piness/transcript?language=en.

Weiss, Allen. "Mindfulness: Paying Attention to What's Really Important." Accessed July 5, 2017. https://www.agingcare.com/articles/mindfulness-paying-attention-to -whats-important-175242.htm.

Wikipedia. "Joan Erikson." Last modified February 17, 2017. https://en.wikipedia.org /wiki/Joan_Erikson.

Winerman, Lea. "A Healthy Mind, a Longer Life." *Monitor* 37, no. 10 (2006): 42. http:// www.apa.org/monitor/nov06/healthy.aspx.

Wood, Natalie O'Donnell. "Colorado's Budget Faces Immediate Pressure from Changing Demographics." December 16, 2016. http://www.bellpolicy.org/research/colorados -budget-faces-immediate-pressure-changing-demographics.

"The World As I See It: An Essay by Einstein." Accessed July 18, 2017. http://history.aip .org/history/exhibits/einstein/essay.htm.

Levy, Becca R. "Mind Matters: Cognitive and Physical Effects of Aging Self-Stereotypes." *Journal of Gerontology: Psychological Sciences* 58, no. 4 (2003): P203–P211. https://doi.org/10.1093/geronb/58.4.P203.

Lindland, Eric, Marissa Fond, Abigail Haydon, and Nathaniel Kendall-Taylor. *Gauging Aging: Mapping the Gaps between Expert and Public Understandings of Aging in America*. Washington, DC: Frameworks Institute, 2015. https://frameworksinstitute.org/assets/files/aging_mtg.pdf.

Martin, Claire. "Aging Well Begins with Being Active, Social and Consciously Contributing to Your Community." *Denver Post*, March 21, 2014, updated April 27, 2016. http://www.denverpost.com/2014/03/21/aging-well-begins-with-being-active-social-and-consciously-contributing-to-your-community/.

McCorkle, Jill. *Life after Life*. Chapel Hill, NC: Algonquin Books, 2013.

Mineo, Liz. "Good Genes Are Nice, But Joy is Better." *Harvard Gazette* April, 11, 2017. http://news.harvard.edu/gazette/story/2017/04/over-nearly-80-years-harvard-study-has-been-showing-how-to-live-a-healthy-and-happy-life/.

Nuland, Sherwin B. *The Art of Aging: A Doctor's Prescription for Well-Being*. New York: Random House, 2008.

Packer, George. "David Halberstam Obituary." Postscript, *New Yorker*, May 7, 2007. http://www.newyorker.com/magazine/2007/05/07/david-halberstam.

Peri, Camille. "What I Wish I'd Known About 'Elderspeak': Psychologist Becca Levy: What a Yale Professor Learned about the Way We Think about and Talk to the Elderly." Accessed July 13, 2017. https://www.caring.com/reflections/becca-levy-reflection.

Powers, William. *Hamlet's Blackberry*. New York: HarperCollins, 2010.

Pyle, Encarnacion. "Ohio's Elderly Forced to Choose between Food or Medicine." *Columbus Dispatch*, May 3, 2015. http://www.dispatch.com/article/20150503/NEWS/305039917.

Ramscar, Michael, Peter Hendrix, Cyrus Shaoul, Petar Milin, Harald Baayen. "The Myth of Cognitive Decline: Non-Linear Dynamics of Lifelong Learning." *Topics in Cognitive Science*, January 13, 2014. https://doi.org/10.1111/tops.12078.

Schachter-Shalomi, Zalman, and Ronald S. Miller. *From Age-ing to Sage-ing: A Revolutionary Approach to Growing Older*. New York: Time Warner Books, 1997.

Scott, Paula Spencer. "Feeling Awe." *Parade*, October 9, 2016. https://parade.com/513786/paulaspencer/feeling-awe-may-be-the-secret-to-health-and-happiness/.

"The Secrets of Aging Well: Live Long and Prosper." *WebMD*, 2002. http://www.webmd.com/healthy-aging/features/secrets-of-aging-well#1.

The Power of Fun

ISBN 978-0-578-49484-5

SDR Consulting & Dave Raymond
West Grove, PA
david@raymondeg.com
daveraymondspeaks.com
Twitter: @emperoroffun
Instagram: emperoroffun

Cover Design by MoonGlade Marketing
Book Interior Design by Planet Ten
Published and Printed in the United States of America

I dedicate this book to my mom,
Suzanne Raymond.

On the shoulders of giants we stand.

Miss you!

-David

THE
POWER
OF FUN

Dave Raymond
2019

Table of Contents

Introduction

"Well, try it on," they told me.

I'll never forget the first time I slid my body into all that fresh fur, glue and foam. It was like a few dozen green shag carpets sewn and glued and wired and stapled together. It took form and when I first laid eyes on it in the early spring of 1978, it reminded me of a second cousin to the Muppets' Miss Piggy.

But six months later, after a hot Philadelphia summer, the new car smell was gone, replaced by … well, you could have dunked that thing in hot water and made perspiration tea. But, that was OK. We had a lot of fun, me and this big, green thing with a 12-inch inflatable tongue, the size 30 shoes and backward red ball cap. That's where Ken Griffey Jr. got the idea, you know. I was a college kid from Newark, Delaware, who needed something to do in the summer and was lucky enough to land a part-time gig with the Philadelphia Phillies. "Just go out and have fun," Bill Giles, my boss and the Phillies executive vice president, told me — and that's what I did.

I followed his orders. They were life changing. And they can be life changing for you.

The Phillie Phanatic — the best, most iconic and, of course, most fun mascot in all of sports — was born on April 25, 1978. For 16 years, I was the guy inside that costume, buzzing around Veterans Stadium on my four-wheeler, terrorizing Tommy Lasorda, mocking umpires, spit-shining bald guys' heads, dancing on dugouts, dropping popcorn (accidentally on purpose) on opposing fans, high-fiving Tug McGraw, visiting hospitals, attending funerals—yep, did that—pushing the envelope and simply following orders.

Spending 16 years inside that big, green costume taught me the Power of Fun and how it can transform a life.

I saw how a Hall of Fame player, the best to ever play his position, finally gained acceptance in Philadelphia the moment he decided to accept fun into his life.

I saw how it put smiles on the faces of fans even when the product on the field wasn't all that good.

I saw how it drove an organization and how having a workplace that was fun actually enhanced productivity.

I saw how it affected my own life and helped me get through the loss of my mother way before we were ready to let go of her.

I saw how it pulled me through the dissolution of my first marriage and ultimately led me to the bliss of my second—even if my brother-in-law didn't immediately approve. You see, my future mother-in-law told him his sister was "dating a Phillie." (OK, so she stretched the facts a little bit.)

Technically, the Phanatic might be a voiceless mass of green fur, but for 16 years and through today, that big green guy was whispering something important and profound in my ear. I want you to hear what I heard all those years ago.

In this book, you will hear some of my best Phanatic stories. And, you will hear the four simple lessons that shag carpet taught me from 1978 up until today. It starts with the F.U.N. of fun.

First, I realized fun can be a Force (F.) if you chose to see it and use it.

Second, I found out that fun can work anywhere. It's a Universal (U.) force that worked in the places you might expect—baseball games and parties—and in places you might not expect—from Bobby and Ethel Kennedy's private residence at Hickory Hill to electric polymer engineering conventions.

Third, I learned to embrace the word "No" (N.)—the battle cry of the Funkiller—and see how this fun could be adapted to work in different environments.

Finally, when I put it all together (F.U.N.), I saw how amazing this universal force, when applied correctly, could be at overcoming some of my worst times. Distracting yourself with fun, to overcome negative brain wiring and help in the worst of times, is where the Power of Fun takes shape and can truly help.

It changed my life. It can change your life.

I call it The Power of Fun.

CHAPTER 1
Just Go Out and Have Fun

"I want you to just go out and have fun."
– Bill Giles
Philadelphia Phillies Vice President 1978

Sports were a central theme in my life while growing up in Newark. I was a pretty good left-handed pitcher and wide receiver at Newark High School. Baseball was my first love, but football wasn't far behind. It couldn't be. My dad, Tubby Raymond, was head coach of the University of Delaware Fighting Blue Hens football team for 36 years. If I might boast a little, he presided over three National Championship teams, won 300 games and was inducted into the College Football Hall of Fame in 1993. As a kid, I remember being allowed into the Blue Hens locker room before games. I remember how captivating my dad's pre-game speeches were, how the players soaked up every word and how they touched me even as a young kid. I dreamed of playing for my dad at Delaware. I wanted to become a coach just like him. I wanted to lead and motivate teams, just like him.

What's funny is my search for that dream led me to the Philadelphia Phillies and all the lessons of The Power of Fun that the big green guy taught me.

I enrolled at Delaware in the fall of 1974 and I was determined to play on my dad's football team. I was too small to catch passes for him, but I had developed into a pretty good kicker in high school and was able to become the starting punter by my junior year. As for the coaching thing, my dad had concerns. He knew it was a tough lifestyle. He warned me I would have to move my family around the country a few times chasing the right jobs and that I'd get fired at least once when it wasn't my fault and once when it was. He did not want me to major in physical education because he believed it would limit me to only teaching and coaching and he knew how tough the coaching gig could be.

At my dad's urging, I became a business major—until I met accounting class. No fun. Good-bye, business major! Hello, phys. ed! Don't tell Dad.

Ultimately, I did tell my dad of my decision to switch majors and he was cool with it. I wanted to coach, and he would help me get started. But first, he wanted to know what I was going to do for a summer job. He mentioned that he would investigate getting me something with the Phillies. Looking back, I will always remember how that conversation ended. "David, you never know who you could meet and what might happen." Turned out Dad must have had an amazing premonition. Like a lot of people who understand the Power of Fun naturally, I would have to label Dad as a true Funster but only after I was finished playing for him. Funster isn't the first thing that comes to mind for Dad as a coach!

Dad had a long connection to the Phillies through the Carpenter family. The Carpenters owned the team from 1943 to 1981 and they were huge supporters of Delaware athletics. My dad's connections with the Carpenters led to me getting an internship with the Phillies in the summer of 1976.

Little did I know how it would shape my life.

The summer of 1976 was a big one in Philadelphia. The city put on its Sunday best for the nation's Bicentennial celebration and the Phillies were a big part of it. They hosted Major League Baseball's All-Star Game in July so there was a ton of work for me to help out with during what I thought would be one summer with the club. I made sure there were plenty of All-Star ballots around for fans. I collected ballots, boxed them, weighed them and sent them off to MLB headquarters. Sometimes, I even got to shag fly balls in batting practice. Tug McGraw complimented my curveball one day. I think he meant it, too. Either that or he was just trying to make me feel good. Tug was an All-Star Funster and knew all about the power of a smile—and putting one on someone's face.

I was assigned to the promotions office that summer and worked under Frank Sullivan, a wonderful, happy, fun-loving man with an infectious laugh. Frank was colorblind so his wife had to pick out his clothes. I worked closely with two great women who are still with the Phillies, Chrissy Long and Adele MacDonald. We always knew when Frank dressed himself because he showed up with mismatched socks. It was always worth a good laugh. Thinking back, the Phillies offices were filled with laughter in those days. The organization cultivated a culture of fun that was way ahead of its time. Long before the dot-com era when young CEOs began to use play and fun to relieve stress and increase productivity during work, the Phillies front office understood their work as marketing a game and marketing fun! It was vital that they enjoyed what they did. Sometimes their marketing gimmicks went awry like the not-so-great ostrich race between Richie Ashburn and Harry

Kalas that summer, but all in all, things went well, and I loved that summer. The Phillies had five players on the All-Star team, they won the National League East and I had a front row seat to all of it. Little did I realize then, but I had become part of the Phillies family and fun was the family business. Everything I learned would help me become a bigger part of the fun in the days to come.

I returned to the Phillies and Veterans Stadium in the summer of 1977, but, frankly, with the buzz of the Bicentennial having come and gone, there wasn't as much to do for an intern in the promotions department. Oh, I made my contributions that summer—the cow-chip throwing contest comes to mind—but I feared I would not be asked back for the summer of 1978 simply because there wasn't a need for me. I remember the feeling of disappointment I had after that season. I had gotten to know the players well and felt for them after the devastating Black Friday loss to the Dodgers in the National League Championship Series. I was also sad because I thought I was walking out of the Vet for the last time. As I headed back to UD for my senior year, I did not see how the Phillies would have a need for me the following summer. Thank goodness I was wrong.

One day in early March 1978, I returned to my fraternity house after taking an exam and one of my frat brothers told me that the Phillies had called twice and wanted me to call back. I was in no rush to return the call because I knew they were just going to tell me that unfortunately, I wouldn't be able to have my job back that summer. I waited a while to call back, hoping that suddenly they would realize how valuable my ostrich-wrangling abilities and cow-chip tossing skills were. Finally, I dialed the number and got through to Chrissy.

"Whatever you do, David, just say no!" she said with a laugh.

I was curious.

Frank Sullivan got on the line and asked if I wanted my summer internship back.

I was overjoyed. I told him that I feared he was calling to tell me that they didn't want me back. He laughed. He knew he had me.

"Of course, we want you back," he said. "It wouldn't be the same without our favorite intern."

I sensed I was being buttered-up for something, but I was cool with it. Another summer of fun? I loved that internship. Frank kept laying it on.

"How would you like to stay for all the home games? And get paid," he said.

I was cool with that. I stayed for most of the games anyway. It was a great perk. But now I'd be paid? My mind raced with excitement and a little bit of confusion. In one side of my head, I could hear Chrissy saying, "Just say no!" In the other side … well, excitement won this debate.

"Frank, I'm all in! What do you want me to do?"

For many years, the Phillies had a couple of mascots, cute little colonial folks named Phil and Phyllis. Well, they had been given their unconditional release. Bill Giles, the man who had been at the forefront in promoting the wondrous Astrodome earlier in his career, had contacted Jim Henson, the creator of the Muppets. Henson connected the Phillies with Bonnie Erickson. She was one of Henson's original designers and just the person who could freshen up the Phillies' tired mascot. Things had moved fast. Frank explained the concept to me on the phone that day and said they needed someone to go to New York to be fitted for the costume. That someone was me!

The Muppets.

Jim Henson.

A new Phillies mascot.

I was so excited that it never entered my mind that maybe I was the only one in the organization dumb enough to say yes to this "opportunity."

"What's it going to look like?" I asked Frank, breathlessly.

"Well, it'll be a big, fat, green bird with a long trumpet-like nose," he told me with a giggle.

I listened. And listened. And pondered. I got to thinking about how Philadelphia fans would boo Santa Claus and the Easter Bunny. A big, fat, green bird with a trumpet-like nose. I thought about it some more. I thought about the booing some more. I was skeptical … but, hey, I had just gotten my job back with the Phillies! I was all in. A big, fat, green bird with a trumpet-like nose. All-righty-then. Why didn't I think of that?

The organization shared some of my concerns about how the new mascot would be accepted by the region's discerning fans. But Bill Giles was not afraid of a few Funkillers. (Funkillers? Stay with me and we will get to them.) Later that week, I was off to Bonnie Erickson's studio in the garment district of New York City to be fitted.

Bonnie was to the Phanatic what Betsy Ross was to the Stars and Stripes. It took her and her crew about a month to construct the costume that Bill Giles had dreamed up—the big, fat, green bird with the trumpet-like nose we now know as the Phanatic.

The creature got its name simply enough. The motto for the 1978 season was *Be a Phillie Phanatic!* So, meet The Phillie Phanatic! To be honest, there were skeptics of the name and the design and the whole concept itself. Many of those skeptics were in-house. Was the design too … out there? Was it too … silly? Would fans connect with a mascot that had no visual connection to Philadelphia? What would Philadelphia's notoriously tough sporting press say? All of these concerns were weighed, but Bill and Frank and the rest of the Funsters at Veterans Stadium pressed on with the idea and the project. Bonnie and her crew sewed and stapled and glued in New York and the Funsters in Philadelphia turned their attention to figuring out the best way to introduce the new mascot. Finally, after much debate, it was decided that there would be no introduction at all. Someone grabbed a pocket schedule and circled the date April 25. The Chicago Cubs were in town. That would be the night the Phanatic would just appear.

Show up. Have fun. See what happens.

Of course, there was some major anxiety even beyond concerns of whether the beast would be accepted by the fans. The costume was supposed to be long finished but there were some last-minute delays and it wasn't delivered to the Vet until the morning of the 25th.

I will never forget the feeling that I had that day. I was nervous when I arrived at the Vet early that afternoon. I darted up to Frank's office and the nervousness turned to excitement. There it was, hanging on a coat rack in all its green, furry majesty. The costume looked just like the drawings said it would—no stiff, lifeless plaster head or cheap-looking body suit. This looked like it jumped right off the television screen and the Muppet Show and everyone agreed. The costume had passed the eye test, at least among the assembled Funsters who had dreamed it up. Maybe this could work.

I couldn't wait to slip into the costume, and when I did, it fit like a tailored suit. I was surprised how much movement I had. I looked like a giant green Muppet, but I could move, dance, jump and wrestle with Tommy Lasorda if I had to. It was still early in the day on April 25, the day the Phanatic was born, and the gates hadn't opened yet. Wearing my new fur, I waddled out into the ballpark and down section 235 to the field where some players were taking early batting practice. My new friend and I passed an early test because all of the players had a good laugh at the new mascot— and they were surprised to hear it was me inside. I posed for a few pictures, including one with infielder turned coach Tony Taylor. He was one of my all-time favorites, a kind and happy man who always had a smile on his face—a man, you could say, who knew the Power of Fun.

As game time approached that night, I realized I had no specific direction on what I was supposed to do. I had an idea of what I wanted the Phanatic's personality to be, high-energy, a little hyper, with a splash of my favorite cartoon characters and maybe a little Three Stooges mixed in. In my mind's eye, the Phanatic would be Daffy Duck, flying around frenetically one second and planting a big, wet kiss on someone's forehead the next. It was opening night and I had been given the role of a lifetime. But I had no script, no real understanding of this new character.

I went off to find the Phanatic's dad.

"Mr. Giles, what is it that you want the Phanatic to do?" I asked.

The look on Mr. Giles' face was not one that I expected. His hand went to his chin. He pondered and pondered ... to the point where I started to get a little nervous. Finally, a huge smile crossed his face and the words that have long inspired me across every platform of life came off his tongue.

"David, I want you to just go out and have fun tonight," he said. "Make sure you have fun. If you're not having fun then the Phanatic will not be funny and the fans won't like him."

I breathed a sigh of relief. I could feel my confidence and excitement levels rise. I was a college kid, right? I was a fan of the Three Stooges and Daffy Duck, right? I had some expertise in having fun and my boss had just told me that it was my job, my primary directive, in fact, to have fun. I got this! I pulled on my big green head, adjusted the trumpet nose and charged out of Bill's office. I was so excited and focused on having fun that I only caught a few syllables of his final directive.

"G-rated fun, David! G-rated fun!" Bill shouted as I ran out of his office.

OK, got it, family fun it is!

And fun is what I had for sure. So did the Phillies organization and, of course, those Philadelphia fans. That first year proved that the Phillies fans could accept a 300-pound, green, furry Muppet as their mascot. Not only did they accept him, but they have embraced him over 40 years as one of the most beloved figures in Philadelphia sports history. It can be argued that the Phanatic has also become the mascot for the city of Philadelphia. How could an idea that looked to be doomed before it started become successful beyond anyone's imagination?

Lesson One: F.
The Force of Fun

I have come to believe it was Bill's simple directive to "just have fun" that allowed the Phillie Phanatic to succeed at first and then grow into the most successful mascot in all of sports. The Force of Fun allowed the Phillies to create a marketing initiative whose job it was to distract the customers from what they were selling. Imagine that?

What if your bosses let you know, above all else, that they wanted you to first have fun while you were at work?

It is also important to note that your boss isn't crazy for giving you this directive. Enlightened leaders know what their culture means to success on the balance sheet. Once fun is valued by leadership, employees are happier when they come to work, more engaged with co-workers and healthier, which means fewer sick days to keep employees out of work. Productivity increases and bottom-line success follows.

Once your leader directs you to have fun at work, I guarantee you will never underestimate the Force of Fun again. Just pretend that you are like a Jedi Knight and this force is all around you. All you have to do is recognize it, value it and engage it. Once we do that, Fun becomes easy to engage and like my first day of "Being the Phanatic" you can understand the Force of Fun!

CHAPTER 2

The Phanatic in Church

"It's all right with the priest so I assume
it's OK with God. Let's do it!"

– The Phanatic in Church, 1981

What is the problem with relaxing and having a good time? Most likely nothing as long as it is at the right time and place. OK, good … got it. But who decides when it is the right time to enjoy ourselves? When we are young, it is our parents, and as we get older, it is our bosses, peers and friends. When we become old enough not to care what anyone thinks, we decide when it is time to have fun, right? If you don't believe me just Google "The Villages" and you can experience it live, but that is another story.

Anyway, our leaders and role models guide us and most of us follow. What about the role that society plays in that decision? Well, simply put, we are conditioned to know when is the right time to work and when is the right time to play. I was lucky to have had leaders early in my career with the Phillies who believed in and

supported fun and they always enjoyed their work. I couldn't sepa-
rate the fun from the work because all of it was fun to me. I couldn't
wait to get to work! I believe that in order to be successful in your
business and personal endeavors, you must be looking for and
embracing fun everywhere. Without fun in all parts of your life,
you will be missing opportunities to grow financially, emotionally
and spiritually.

After the Phanatic was first introduced in April of 1978, something very unexpected happened. The Phillies fans accepted him as
their mascot almost overnight. The Phillies beat the Cubs the night
of the Phanatic's birth and in the paper the next day Tim McCarver
exclaimed, "Hey, we're 1 and 0 with the Phanatic!" I can remember
reading that and being overwhelmed that the Philadelphia sports
media felt that the Phanatic's arrival was significant enough to
include that quote. The fear held by many in the front office about
the Phanatic becoming an embarrassing bust and just another
failed "wacky" promotional stunt was completely extinguished the
very next day. (Thank you, Tim McCarver!)

I believe if the Phillies had included the fans in the decision
to create the Phanatic by releasing concept images of the proposed
mascot, it most surely would have failed.

The Philadelphia 76ers learned that tough lesson in 2012 when
their operating partner, Adam Aron, decided to release three
proposed 76er mascot designs from Jim Henson's company to the
Philadelphia fans. One was a moose, one was a dog, and the final
concept was none other than Ben Franklin himself! The Philadelphia fans answered the Sixers' attempt to direct them by showering
them with boos, catcalls and "thumbs down" emojis through every
social media outlet available. The Lesson: Don't try to tell the
diehard Philadelphia fans what their mascot will be! Have the faith

in your creative process and people to develop a mascot to represent your organization and its ideals and stand behind it.

Hey ... trust the process! Trust *your* process.

By the way, and while we are on this subject, please don't put me in the category of those "Philadelphia fan bashers" that are out there, including the national media and "talking head" pundits. There are no more enthusiastic, knowledgeable or passionate sports fans anywhere in the country than right here in Philadelphia! It's just that you must treat their knowledge and passion with respect and tread lightly when marketing to them. Adam Aron believed he was doing just that with his three-headed mascot roll out. Looking back, he should have had the faith in his people and their creative process to just build it, trust it and stand behind it. Once the Philly sports fans smell that it isn't authentic, they will turn on you like a rabid dog! It is so funny to see that played out today with the 76ers experience because it validated the fear that the Phillies had over 30 years earlier. Tough lesson but one, thankfully, the Phillies didn't have to learn in 1978.

The Phanatic's overnight success was, in large part, due to the brilliant mind of Bill Giles. He was practicing what he learned early in his career while helping to build the wondrous Astrodome in Houston. There really isn't anyone who compares to Bill with regards to his marketing genius. Millions of Phillies fans were born in the '80s because of the fun Bill developed at the Vet. It drew families in. Bill understood how to use entertainment to build young fans who would soon become devoted to baseball. The Phanatic's creation was his master stroke, but he was simply following the first lesson of Fun (the F. in F.U.N.) and doing it naturally, as we saw in Chapter One.

So, I believe the Philadelphia fans were led by that lesson and ultimately embraced the Phanatic as their own, on their own, and not because the Phillies organization orchestrated it. The result was sports promotions magic!

The Phanatic became such a success that requests began coming in to have him appear outside of Veterans Stadium. We didn't even know what the Phanatic was doing in the stadium! What was he going to do at a mall or a car dealership? This was an unusual request in 1978. Guerilla marketing wasn't yet in vogue. Players made personal appearances for fees or as part of their contracts, *but the mascot?* This was so unexpected that for the first Phanatic appearance requests, the Phillies simply took contact information and told clients they would have to get back to them. Bill Giles, of course, was happy to spread the Phanatic's brand of fun outside the Vet.

"Just go out and see what happens and have fun," he told me. Communicating appearance details like the need for a secure dressing area, security support and access to water (it's hot in there!) were not thought of before my first appearances. I would arrive at these events looking like Santa Claus because the costume had a giant red bag so I could transport the Phanatic incognito from place to place. Dressing in a hot public restroom or a broom closet was the norm during this "discovery" phase of Phanatic promotions. I guess you could call it the Wild West of mascotting!

One of my first memories of this type of appearance was at a car dealership in New Jersey. It was on a spring weekend and over 1,000 people showed up. The response was overwhelming and the dealership was completely unprepared. It was crazy! I was truly concerned about the costume and my safety. The Phanatic was mobbed at these appearances. One appearance, at a strip mall on Rt. 202 in

Wilmington, Delaware, had to be canceled because a person in a wheelchair was toppled over by a surging crowd trying to get to the Phanatic. I remember being very nervous trying to explain to Chrissy that we needed to figure out how to protect the Phanatic (and me!) at these appearances. I was just an intern, after all, and I didn't want to lose my job. As it turned out, they were as concerned as I was, and over time, Chrissy did an unbelievable job organizing an entire Phanatic booking process, including paperwork that is still used today. I know she will hate me saying this, but she really became the Phanatic's surrogate mom. And what a great mom she was. All these years later, she still works for the Phillies, specializing in spreading the Power of Fun to millions of fans per year.

In the early '80s, I was performing as the Phanatic at all 81 home games, and making over 200 personal appearances all over the Delaware Valley, as well. Car dealerships, bar mitzvahs, holiday fairs, corporate functions or just about any kind of neighborhood gathering where an appearance by the Phanatic would make it more fun. The biggest surprise to me was the diversity of the requests. It seemed as if there was no event where a Phanatic appearance couldn't be included. I performed at a funeral. Yes, I said it, a funeral! Or should I say an Irish wake? It was for a huge Phillies fan who had passed away in his late 80s and wanted his funeral to be fun. One of his wishes was for the Phanatic to attend his wake. I'll be honest, it wasn't an event that I was looking forward to. What was I supposed to do? What were they expecting of the Phanatic? As it turned out, everyone was having a lot of fun even before the Phanatic arrived, so it felt just like a great big party. The Phanatic walked in to an explosion of chants. Dancing and adult beverages set the tone and I remember thinking as I packed up to leave, "I just entertained at a funeral dressed as a Muppet!" It started to get me thinking that if fun could work at a funeral, where else could it work?

Over my 16 years as the Phanatic, I began to realize that the answer to that question was … everywhere! I performed at a General Electric Polymer Engineers convention in Saratoga Springs, New York. What, you are asking, could I possibly be doing there? Well, I can tell you that on the drive up to Saratoga Springs, I didn't have the answer. It was in the middle of winter and upstate New York was covered in snow. All of my appearances were screened by Chrissy and I rarely questioned her. Bill Giles had taught me well. "Just take the Phanatic out and have fun," he would say. Chrissy would usually give me a quick overview of the appearance and hand me some driving directions. How I wish I had Google Maps and Waze in those days.

It was a little bit out of the ordinary for me to have to drive 300 miles to an appearance, so I was supposed to check in with my contact the night before the event. It was a three-day conference and I would be staying for the entire event. I knew that Chrissy had vetted this group, but it was GE, for crying out loud! I assumed that there were going to be Phillies fans or some connection to base-ball. Maybe it was going to be a baseball/sports themed event and the Phanatic would be a surprise guest. All I knew was that I had the best job in the world and these folks were paying to have the Phanatic drive all the way to Saratoga Springs and entertain them. I didn't give a lot of thought to who I was going to entertain at this event, though it did occur to me that most likely everyone attending would be an adult.

Entertaining adults motivated me when I started performing. The Phillies received many requests for the Phanatic to attend events that were largely for adults in part because of what they saw the Phanatic doing at the Phillies games. The desire to get reaction from adults came from my need to be accepted by the major league players. One of the thrills for me when I became the Phanatic was the realization that I was going to have access to the Phillies players. Think about it. The biggest reason my friends were envious of my work as the Phanatic was my ability to walk up to any major league ballplayer and pretty much "clown" around with them as if I were a friend or teammate! My job, of course, gave me access to all the visiting team players, as well. This unfettered access to major league ballplayers was the best and most memorable part of my job. I got to pretend that I was one of them, and if I got a response from a player while I was performing, I felt like I really had accomplished something. In a sense, it made me feel like I had realized the dream of becoming a major league player. It drove me to become good at entertaining the players on the field, and as a result, all of the adult fans in the stands. The folks in the seats liked living vicariously through the Phanatic's antics. One of the main reasons adult sports fans love the Phanatic is because he entertains their children. That was not my focus at all. As I saw it, entertaining children was easy. They, after all, are natural Funsters. They want to play all the time and it was so simple to make them happy with a wave or a hug and it wasn't difficult to get them to respond. On the other hand, professional athletes, in many ways, are jaded and don't let their guard down very often, so when I got them to laugh or respond to the Phanatic I felt like I had accomplished something.

So, as I drove up to Saratoga Springs that long ago winter day, I knew that I would be in my element with adults, but I didn't know what they were expecting of me. When I arrived and talked to my contact, it became clear that they were hoping the Phanatic could provide simple comic relief to a series of meetings that were to be exceptionally intense. GE had newly-hired research chemists and scientists come together to meet about issues that they were having with research and development. During these meetings they had challenges that required innovative and or creative solutions. If they did not come up with solutions to the problems at hand, they could quite possibly lose their jobs. It would be a very stressful few days and they were hoping the Phanatic could use his brand of spontaneous entertainment to distract and entertain them during their breaks. Looking back, this was a perfect example of a big corporation using the Power of Fun to increase the productivity of its employees! GE and Jack Welch were way ahead of their time. The best part of this assignment was I only had to work about 30 minutes in the morning and then about an hour during the cocktail party later in the evening each day! I worked in the morning then headed to Gore Mountain to ski for the rest of the day before returning just in time for the evening party. The most amazing part of this was how happy those GE people were with my work. *Work?* I really wasn't sure what "work" I was doing.

The first meeting of the morning ended just as breakfast was served. I decided that I would put a Chef's hat on the Phanatic's head and come out of the kitchen with a tray of covered dishes. They were piled ridiculously high and, on cue, the Phanatic walked about 10 paces, tripped, fell and let the dishes crash to the ground, making the perfect thunderous entrance to announce his arrival at the conference. The Phanatic was well received and he set a positive tone because the attendees would be waiting to see how the big, green guy would arrive after each of their meetings. After entering, the Phanatic was challenged with hugging and goosing as many of the conference goers as possible. How could you not be happy with that "work?"

As I was driving home that week, I remember saying to myself, "You just entertained rocket scientists dressed as a Muppet!" It was difficult to wrap my mind around it. How could this work actually be effective on clients? I didn't fret over the answer because I was just thrilled with the week, and I felt a special feeling of accomplishment because of the heartfelt thanks that the people running the event gave me as I finished. Any fear of an appearance going horribly wrong, no matter how strange the request, slowly started to fade with each successful event.

No appearance was more frightening than when the Phanatic was invited to a Catholic Church breakfast in Cinnaminson, New Jersey, in early 1984. When I received the request and followed the normal process of booking the event, there was nothing unusual about it at all. It was a father, son and daughter breakfast to be held before Mass on a Sunday at Saint Charles Borromeo, a parish filled with Phillies fans in Cinnaminson. This was the type of appearance that I had grown very accustomed to because it involved families gathering to eat a meal and celebrate. It was unstructured with regard to the Phanatic's participation because they would leave it up to me to spontaneously entertain them by going table to table, kissing, hugging and taking pictures along the way. I was expecting to work in costume for about an hour and head back home as the Mass would start after the breakfast event. What I didn't expect was being asked to stick around by a man who has since become one of the best and most inspirational friends I've ever made.

I had just finished working the breakfast, and I was in the break room about to get completely out of the Phanatic costume. A Deacon with the church that had been acting as my spotter was in the break room. This was always one of the most uncomfortable times working as the Phanatic. There's not much dignity in taking off the Phanatic's head, unzipping the body, dropping it down to my knees, completely drenched with sweat and then sitting down as if I was on the toilet asking some stranger to grab me a towel. I would have a small bucket of ice water next to me with a plastic bag for all my sweat-soaked T-shirts. It was refreshing to strip off the wet T-shirt and be shirtless in the air conditioning because it would help me to cool off faster. But I had to do all of this in front of people that I had just met.

On this Sunday afternoon, the Deacon came into my dressing room as I was about to take the costume off. He asked if I could wait for a few minutes because the Youth Minister at St. Charles wanted to ask a favor of me. "Sure," I said, and I put a dry T-shirt on and combed my hair, trying to look as presentable as possible. I was expecting a venerable old priest with a white collar and a flowing robe to enter the room. Much to my surprise, a few minutes later a very young-looking man in a colorful short-sleeved shirt came bounding into the room, grabbed my hand, shook it vigorously and said, "Hi, David! My name is Father Jim Dever and I am the Youth Minister here at St. Charles. I was wondering if you could do a big favor for me."

"Well, sure Father Dever. What is it that you would like me to do?" I asked.

It's so hard for me to explain how inspiring Father Jim can be unless you have had the pleasure of knowing him. His face is always so full of joy and enthusiasm. Just his voice and inflection are soothing, but at the same time motivating. It was the first of many times that I would look into that face for calm reassurance. Jim grew up in the Kensington section of Philadelphia, the only son of Walter and Ruth Dever. He attended North Catholic High School and because of his strong sense of service to others, joined the Seminary while still in high school. He was ordained a priest in 1973. He has an undergraduate degree in Theology and English from Catholic University and Allentown College. He also attended Villanova, where he received a graduate degree in Fine Arts. Most importantly he is, in my mind, a Funster of the highest degree!

As I changed out of my costume that day in Cinnaminson, Jim told me he was about to say Mass. He asked if the Phanatic would be willing to do something unusual but fun. He wanted the Phanatic to sneak into the chapel behind him and the altar boys as Mass was about to start. As much as I wanted to honor Father Jim's request, I was at first a little frightened. His request reminded me of a moment from my youth. When I was 10, I was asked to be an acolyte at my family's Methodist church in Newark. The job required me to dress in traditional altar boy robes and light all the candles in the chapel 10 minutes before the service began. Once the service was over, I would come back in the chapel and extinguish the candles. This petrified me because I feared I might knock the candles over and light the entire church on fire! I told my mom how frightened I was to be an acolyte and she gave me great advice that I still listen to today and have told my kids many times as they have grown up. She said, "David, just being afraid is not a good enough reason not to try something that you could be proud of." As I heard my mother's voice in my head, Jim studied the puzzled look on my face.

"Father Dever," I said, "I'm not sure this is a good idea. I mean, I'm not Catholic, and I am really not sure of the Phanatic's denomination and this is church! Should the Phanatic really be sneaking into church to disrupt Sunday Mass?"

A huge and wonderful smile broke across Father Dever's face and he said, "David, this will be perfect! You see, my homily this morning is all about how life can surprise us with a curveball or two and the Phanatic's unanticipated visit will set the tone for that message. It will be powerful and memorable! Please help me do that for my congregation."

There was no getting out of this. Mom and Father Dever were united in their belief that this was a perfectly good idea. I guess I was on board after I realized that if it would be all right with the priest then I am sure the Lord would be supportive. So, who was I to be the Funkiller?

"Let's go do this thing!" I said.

A few minutes later, there was the Phanatic heading into the St. Charles chapel filled with over 150 parishioners. I could see Father Dever and the altar boys walking down the long aisle toward the altar. I was surprised by the sheer volume of people. I wasn't expecting that. I couldn't see any of the parishioner's faces because we were entering from the back of the church and they were focused on Father Dever and his procession.

From the back of the church, I quietly began creeping up the aisle about 30 paces behind the procession. I felt like the Phanatic and I were sneaking toward a very special moment. I was excited and confident about that because I was given permission by both Father Jim and God! After all, the Phanatic had successfully entertained at a funeral so how could this be any more difficult? I was soon to find out.

For the most part, at any function where I had performed as the Phanatic and was introduced, those in attendance would let out a huge roar of acceptance. Many times, they would break into spontaneous cheers and laughter or yell, "Go Phillies!" It was the response that I had grown to expect, but given that I was now sneaking into a Catholic Mass, I wasn't sure what to expect at St. Charles that day, and I certainly wasn't prepared for what I heard.

As I crept down the aisle passing the first few pews, the startled parishioners slowly took their attention away from Father Jim's procession and looked back toward the Phanatic. I started to hear a very disturbing sound. I can only describe it as the sucking in of air followed by muffled and distressed mumbling. I am sure if we were not in church there would have been a scream or two from the older women in the chapel. When I was passing each pew, the mumbling became coherent and they were saying, "What is HE doing in HERE!?" and, "This isn't where HE should BE!" And, of course, right out of a Dr. Seuss book, some of them quietly told the Phanatic, "Stop. Stop … You must get OUT of HERE before the priest sees YOU!"

My first instinct was to listen to them and high-tail it out of there, but I guess they didn't realize *I was a professional*. I knew what I was doing and I was halfway down the main aisle and, frankly, I was doing what Father Dever had wanted. I was throwing one heck of a curveball at them! The stunned mumbling of the congregation continued to grow as the Phanatic sneaked his way up to the altar. The altar boys peeled off and headed to their seats as Father Jim turned to face the congregation with outstretched arms. That was my perfect opening because as Father Jim made that turn, I caught up with him. Without hesitation, I reached up and grabbed him behind his neck, stuck the Phanatic's giant feathered nose over his face and made a loud kissing sound. I then released him, turned around and started to run as fast as I could back down the aisle that I had just moments earlier sneaked up. I was running not for comic effect but in raw fear. I assumed that all the astonished parishioners who had just witnessed the green guy accost their beloved priest would form a mob and scream, "Kill the monster!" and like Dr. Frankenstein's creation, the Phanatic would be doomed. Thank God they didn't have access to picks, torches and clubs!

As I ran down the aisle, I noticed that the looks of abject horror had slowly started to change to smiles, and as I got further down the aisle, I could hear laughter. And as I got to the end of the aisle and turned toward the side door of the chapel for my escape, I heard cheering and chants of, "Go Phanatic … Go Phillies!" I looked over my shoulder to see Father Jim smiling, laughing and cheering, and it occurred to me that the parishioners were experiencing what I had experienced 20 minutes earlier: It's all right with Father Dever, it's all right with God, so it's cool with us. "Let's go Phillies … Let's go Phanatic!"

Once again, as I drove home from this appearance, I said to myself, "I just entertained at a Catholic Mass dressed as a Muppet!" It became clear to me that there was virtually no event that the Phanatic couldn't successfully add entertainment value to. And it continues today. I remain great friends with Tom Burgoyne, the Phanatic's current best friend, and he told me the story about how the Phanatic entertained inside the Supreme Court Justice's private chambers!

What?! That's right.

When Justice Samuel Alito was confirmed onto the Supreme Court bench, his fellow Justices wanted his welcome to be special and memorable. A visit from the big, green guy did the trick. Justice Alito hails from Trenton, New Jersey and is a big Phillies fan. Upon his arrival at the Supreme Court that night, the Phanatic danced his way into the court's private chambers to the rousing approval of the people entrusted with protecting our Constitution! Just for a moment, the Phanatic joined and entertained the greatest legal minds in our nation with his simple brand of slapstick humor!

Without realizing it, the Phillies created probably the best ambassador, not only for the team, but the city of Philadelphia as well. From a marketing perspective, nothing is more valuable to your brand than a character that drives your message against a positive backdrop of memorable and sometimes hilarious entertainment. In the case of the Phanatic, he subtly delivered the message that there was more than baseball going on at a Phillies game. He delivered fun to thousands of families in the Delaware Valley, including some who really were not baseball fans. His impact transcended baseball and still does today. People buy Phillies tickets because they want to see the Phillies win but there will always be fans who bought their tickets to just see the Phanatic. So, good for the Phillies—and good for the GE Polymer Engineers and the Catholics in Cinnaminson, as well.

But what does this mean for you? It's a great question and it brings us to the second lesson of Powerful Fun.

Lesson 2: U.
Universal – Fun Works Anywhere

Goals can be reached faster, initiatives can be more successful, events can be more impactful and messages will be more memorable when you insert a piece of appropriate fun. A dose of fun works everywhere. If it works at a funeral, where would it not work?

When facing a challenge or struggle, one of the most important questions to ask is: "Where is the fun?" Think of it this way: We have long been conditioned to seek out or create fun only on our "off" time because we see fun as appropriate only during times that we are relaxing and happy. We have a tendency to avoid fun when we are at work or dealing with challenges.

At work and during times of great focus, or even when emotionally challenged, we do not believe that fun belongs. This is why this second lesson is so powerful once you believe it, value it and practice it. We must see fun as a piece of the overall solution to many of the problems we face in business and life.

I remember listening to Steve O, famous for his work in the *Jackass* movies, on the Howard Stern show one day. Stern asked Steve O why his outrageous antics seemed to strike a chord in a very diverse demographic of fans. "We are distraction therapists practicing distraction therapy!" Steve O exclaimed. I love that quote and it resonates with me because the Phanatic has been practicing distraction therapy since he was born!

The insertion of an unexpected dose of fun will always distract us from our current struggles and problems and when we are distracted our guard is down and unexpected solutions can be discovered.

You don't necessarily need to be a "Jackass" to be a Funster. Just remember the power of distraction therapy. It all starts with asking the question: "Where is the fun?"

CHAPTER 3
The Battle Cry of the Funkiller

"I had no idea you were a professional idiot."
– Los Angeles High School Band Director

From the time the Phanatic was born in 1978 he was a big success. He delivered powerful fun because the Phillies let him. It wasn't until he and I ventured out into the public that we started to hear the word "No!" In time, I began to call this the battle cry of the Funkiller.

Without Bill Giles' leadership there is no question that the Phanatic would have never been born and, believe me, there was no shortage of input from Funkillers. Bill fended them off by continually saying, "this is going to be fun," and the Phillies really needed fun during the late '70s. Veterans Stadium was still new and the promotions philosophy was best described as: The wackier the better! It was working and each year Bill Giles and Frank Sullivan worked very hard to deliver as much silliness as possible. They were true Funsters and never let the voice of the Funkiller slow them down. It is important to mention that they didn't ignore that input. Actually, they welcomed it because they knew many of their superiors were Funkillers and it was important for their livelihood that the fun being planned would be safe, appropriate and successful. Kite Man and The Great Wallendas notwithstanding.

In most cases, the Funkiller voice is coming from leadership or from a position of experience and that voice needs to be respected. What was beautiful about the Phillies leadership, which included owners Bob and Ruly Carpenter, was that they gave their input and concerns then stepped back and let Bill, Frank and the promotions staff do their jobs and have their fun. They even let them fail and only said, "I told you so," during the post-game debrief (OK, they were cocktail hours) and only because they had so much fun ribbing Bill and Frank for the latest crazy promotion gone awry. Even though I didn't recognize it at the time, this trait was an indication that the Phillies executives were great leaders. They fueled the creative energy that lead to great ideas. They naturally understood the process of leadership development. The people who were put in charge of ballpark entertainment were a different breed and it was important for their ideas to be championed and valued even if it occasionally led to failure. I guess it's hard to imagine that the voice of a Funkiller can really be a key to the success of Powerful Fun. I know it sounds counterintuitive, but this is a very important component in the Power of Fun. It is probably the single most important lesson of the Power of Fun because if we don't understand and respect it, we will lose the battle even before we arm ourselves. And if you don't think it is a battle, just look at the world around you.

Our society has always put a premium on hearing the bad news first. Whether it is on the nightly news or in the board room, the bad news is always the lead. It is in this environment where the Funkiller's voice is the loudest. But it is also the Funkiller who is trying to protect us. Much like a parent who is trying to keep their children safe. At the same time, good parents recognize failure may be one of the ways for their children to learn how to grow and become successful. This is the quandary of the Funkiller. How do we understand the role of the Funkiller when we want to harness the Power of Fun? How do we use the Funkiller's critical advice to our advantage? How do we make it part of the solution?

The Phanatic has the answer.

Who were my Funkillers while I was the Phanatic? Well, how about opposing fans, players and managers for starters? Grounds keepers were some of the worst Funkillers on the planet for the Phanatic. They also held the least amount of perspective. "If I could just get rid of these idiots wearing spikes, my field would be beautiful," the groundskeeper was heard to say. Believe me, this is not an overstatement. For most of my career, I was lucky because I worked at Veterans Stadium. The field was made of an artificial surface and my antics on the Phanatic's all-terrain vehicle couldn't damage the field the way it would if we had played on natural grass. It certainly is a much different ballgame for my good friend Tom Burgoyne, the current best friend of the Phillie Phanatic. You have no idea the negotiations that had to be held for the Phanatic to continue the tradition of riding his ATV on the grass field at Citizens Bank Park. The Cuban Missile Crisis was easier to solve!

I will never forget the time when I was on the road with the Phanatic in Boise, Idaho. It was in the late '80s and the Phanatic's reputation as a great minor league baseball "act" had grown over the years. In the late '70s, the Phanatic started being invited by all of the Phillies' minor league affiliates. From Portland, Oregon, to

Clearwater, Florida, the Phanatic had become a big draw for our minor league teams. Minor league baseball is a classic study in the Power of Fun. Affiliates really don't have to worry about the product on the field because 90 percent of that operation is funded by their major league team. The "General Manager" position in minor league baseball is not responsible for the players or the field manager. Their responsibility is to sell tickets by producing as much family-oriented fun as possible for their fans and acts like the Phanatic had become part of what minor league fans demanded. Max Patkin, The Clown Prince of Baseball, was a minor league baseball superstar performance comedian and the San Diego Chicken was making the rounds in a decked out touring bus, sparking ticket sales everywhere he went and earning upwards of $10,000 per show in his heyday.

Once the Phillie Phanatic started showing up at Reading Phillies games in 1979, the flood gates opened. Our teams in Clearwater and Spartanburg, South Carolina, were next. The visiting teams that were in town on those nights playing the Phillies' minor league teams would report back to their respective home team's general manager that a strange green, furry Muppet was loose on the field, entertaining the fans and driving ticket sales. It wasn't long before minor league clubs from all over the country came calling. The Phanatic was performing at over 35 minor league games as well as 81 Phillies home games each season, dragging me along with him all the while.

I'm still surprised when I think back on the first minor league game that I performed at where neither team was affiliated with the Phillies. But there the Phanatic was, in all his Greendom, with his size 30 shoes, a Phillies jersey on, belly bumping, dancing, and successfully entertaining baseball fans that had never seen the Phillies play. It made me realize that in the minor leagues, it wasn't all about winning, it was all about having fun. It was my kind of atmosphere—for sure! It was a thrill to take the Phanatic on the road and experience a little bit of that April 1978 debut-night euphoria over and over again.

So that brings us back to Boise and my first showdown with their insane head groundskeeper.

ATVs had become an important part of the Phanatic's act and a fan favorite. Obviously, I couldn't travel with one so I worked with each minor league organization to help them have an ATV, sponsored by a local dealer, on hand for the game. It would be delivered to the stadium a few hours before the game. On this night in Boise, the Boise Hawks' groundskeeper, a man named Joe, was completely unaware that the Phillie Phanatic would be performing, let alone riding an ATV all over his pristine grass field! The reason he was unaware of these facts was because the team's owner and general manager had not informed him. And the reason they had not informed him was because Joe happened to be a crazed, fun-hating lunatic. His bosses were afraid of him! I kid you not.

When I told them of my plans to enter the field on the ATV, they cowered, lowered their heads and told me that I had to clear that with Joe first. "Who's Joe?" I asked. I assumed by their reaction, he must be a co-owner or someone in a decision-making position. When I learned that he was the head groundskeeper, I was surprised and asked them why he had the final say. They responded by telling me he was the best groundskeeper in the business and that I had to know him to understand. I guess it is very hard to grow grass in Boise and a good groundskeeper was hard to find. I told them that I would speak with Joe and get his approval—even though the fun-seeking rebel inside me knew I would be gone the next day, paycheck in hand, so it didn't matter to me what I did to his field.

If he was that good at growing freaking grass, then he could fix any damage I could create in one short night.

I went on to the field to meet with Joe. When I came through the access gate, I saw a guy watering the dirt portion of the infield. It was hot as hell and he had no shirt on. It reminded me of the movie *Top Gun*, and how its writers tried to have Tom Cruise pose without his shirt as much as possible. I found out later that Joe never wore shirts. Oh, great! This should have been a warning to me, but I did not have the extreme pleasure of knowing Joe very well, or at all, for that matter. I walked across the dirt to where he was diligently watering. He looked at me with disdain.

"Can't you see that I'm watering my dirt?" he said.

"Oh, I'm sorry but I just wanted to talk to you about my performance tonight," I replied.

"What performance?" he spat.

I went on to explain who I was and what I usually have the Phanatic do throughout the game. When I mentioned the part about entering the field on the ATV, he jumped down my throat.

"Not on my field, you're not!"

I told him about all the trouble the owner and general manager went through in order to get the ATV and the Phanatic here for the game and that the fans were expecting to see the Phanatic on his ATV. He just shrugged his shoulders and said that it wasn't any of his concern and the only thing he cared about was his field and there was no way he was letting me on the field with that grass-eating ATV. His field? He cared for nothing else? What an ass! Joe had no perspective and, of course, I was young and stupid and no one challenged me! I was going on that field with the Phanatic's ATV come hell or high water!

I held my temper, though, and diplomatically asked what we could work out. I said I understood his fear and he had every right to be concerned about "his" field. What if I could promise to restrict my driving to the dirt warning track? Could I then use the ATV that night? He said that he would have to discuss it with the GM. A bit later, Joe came to see me in the clubhouse and rendered his decision. It would be all right for me to use the ATV, pre-game only, and only if I kept it on the dirt warning track, and I was not allowed anywhere where the grass was growing.

Yeeesss!

Finally, I had my opening to teach this fun-hating SOB a lesson in the Power of Phanatic Phun!

I had spent the last few years becoming proficient at riding these ATVs. I could ride a wheelie (balanced up on the two back wheels) from the outfield all the way to home plate. I could ride on two wheels while turning a complete circle. I really understood how to make the Phanatic look funny driving like a bat out of hell while staying under control. By far, however, the fans' favorite trick was when the Phanatic would jump over the pitcher's mound, Evel Knievel style, just before the start of every game. At the Vet, I would get behind home plate, rev the engine a few times, pop it into gear, haul ass and hit the pitcher's mound at about 35 miles an hour. The momentum would throw the ATV and the Phanatic about 25 feet in the air toward second base, where he would land with a thump and continue off of the field just before the players were announced. It was a big hit for the fans but a nightmare for the groundskeeper. The mound was a sacred place and pitchers were very picky about how their mound was groomed before their starts. Again, I was lucky to be working in Philadelphia where virtually all of the grounds crew were friends of mine and they loved the mound jump even more than I did.

This was not the case, of course, when the Phanatic was on the road. Most of the time, I would not tell the head groundskeeper that I was going to do it, figuring it was better to seek forgiveness than ask for permission (that's a mascot performer's credo, by the way). But for Joe, the grumpy groundskeeper in Boise, I had something special planned.

When they introduced the Phanatic that night, it was about 20 minutes before first pitch and the stands were full. I was really excited because it was the first time these fans would ever see the Phanatic and it was always a rush to come riding out in front of new fans, jump off the ATV, stick the Phanatic's belly out and start dancing to some great music to show them, right from the start, that it was going to be fun that night. I was careful to stay right on the dirt warning track, just like grumpy Joe had instructed. I didn't even go very fast and when I stopped the ATV, I had it positioned just to the home plate side of the batting circle. This, of course, was all under the watchful eye of Joe, the head groundskeeper. Much to my delight, I saw the owner and general manager of the team were also on the field smiling and enjoying the Phanatic's antics. I had a feeling they were going to enjoy the special surprise I had planned for Joe.

Once the umpires finished with the pre-game meeting at home plate, the national anthem singer was announced and the umps and the Phanatic lined up and stood at attention. Once the national anthem was over, I grabbed the umpire next to me, laid a big, wet, furry kiss on his face then jumped on my ATV. I turned the ignition on and revved the engine a few times. The crowd was still laughing because I had just romantically accosted the home plate umpire, but my attention was focused on Joe who was staring at me like a prison guard, as I sat on the ATV. I broke character for a moment and yelled, "Hey, Joe, watch this! You better get your hose ready!" With that, I popped the ATV into first gear and jammed down on the throttle. Dirt shot up in two streams from each tire and I turned in the direction of Joe's beloved pitcher's mound. The ATV popped up into a wheelie and lurched toward the mound at full speed. The home team's pitcher that day had just reached the mound when he saw the Phanatic coming his way. He jumped back from the mound and as the ATV hit the mound, I remember him yelling something at Joe. The Phanatic landed a few feet in front of second base and came to a stop in the base path between second and first. For good measure, I pretended to be Jeff Gordon after winning a NASCAR race and carved a few doughnuts behind second base before I shot off the field to a rousing ovation from the Boise Hawks faithful! The last image of Joe as I rode off of the field, and it is still seared in my mind, was of him standing there, mouth agape in angry disbelief.

The owner and general manager rushed to see me in the clubhouse. They were in hysterics, laughing and slapping me on the back, both exclaiming at the same time that they knew of no one who needed a good kick in the butt more than Joe. Later, I heard that Joe said if I came back on the field with that ATV, he was going to grab his hunting rifle and shoot me right then and there. I had no doubt that he was serious, so I decided that my ATV fun was over for the night. Looking back, my reactions may have been inappropriate, but I wasn't looking for any lessons at the time. It is only now that I understand the true meaning of the Battle Cry of the Funkiller. But why stop here? I have an even better example of how the Funkiller role can be an important part in learning the Power of Fun.

Coming in a very close second as the worst Funkiller that the Phanatic encountered over the years was the dreaded Band Director! During my first few years as the Phanatic, I learned a great deal about the sports promotion business. I mentioned that the Phillies' promotional credo was "The wackier, the better" and that approach helped create fan interest even when the play on the field was not at its best. The Phillies were regarded as a ground-breaking organization when it came to on-field promotions and events. The Flying Wallendas, Kite Man, hot dog eating contests and college bed races were some of the promotions that gained national news coverage and positioned the Phillies as the team to keep pace with if you wanted to succeed in the zany world of sports promotions. Our events and stunts were well organized and well planned, but they went to the next level and became the stuff of promotional legend because we always weaved in small, unique and impromptu surprises that fans came to love and expect. We were way ahead of our time because nowadays the corporate world calls that "value-added" fun. As a result of this consistent culture of unexpected fun, I, as the Phanatic, was afforded a ton of latitude to develop my own material for these promotions and events.

An example of this was when the Phillies invited high school and college bands to entertain in center field before home games. This entertainment was a surprise because you would expect to see bands at a football game, but in the early '80s it was a novelty to see bands perform at a baseball game. It also was a great way of connecting local schools and organizations to Phillies baseball. I always loved inserting the Phanatic's spontaneous antics into pre-game promotions. Neither the fans nor the participants expected these good-natured interruptions, so the results were always surprising and comical.

The unstructured nature of my performance style was difficult for band directors to embrace because "structure" was at the heart of a band's presentation. The Phanatic brought band directors to the brink of a nervous breakdown. All they could see was a giant, green fur ball trying to disrupt their well-rehearsed performance. The fans, on the other hand, were very entertained for that exact same reason. Watching the Phanatic interrupt a well-organized musical performance was a little like watching a furry green bull loose in a china shop. Fans realized the Phanatic's performance was unscripted and they loved living vicariously through him. What would it be like to jump out of their seats, run right up to the pretty baton twirler and blow her a kiss? How would she react? Would the other band members be able to keep a straight face?

I was only trying to entertain myself during these times and I understood what a "regular" Phillies fan was thinking because I, after all, was one of them. I had the chance to live out most every sports fan's fantasy short of being a player. As the Phanatic, I could run onto the field almost any time I wanted. I could hug a player, an umpire or pretty girl and never get thrown out of the stadium or arrested! It was a Walter Mitty existence and there were no boundaries as long as it was, in Bill Giles' words, "G-rated fun."

In many cases the band directors would have preferred that the Phanatic was arrested, but as much as they could be Funkillers, even they became pacified once they saw and heard the reaction of the Philadelphia fans during and after the band's performance. The great bands wouldn't be distracted and, in fact, played off the spontaneous nature of the Phanatic and created a hybrid march that was more entertaining than what was rehearsed. The great bands were great because of the skill and ability of their directors to drill them so well that nothing would prevent them from playing and marching—even if the Phanatic was hellbent on creating chaos. The results were pure entertainment and memorable fun! The fans loved it and band performances became a Phanatic and fan favorite. Even those occasionally rigid band directors started to become believers. They, of course, were from the Philadelphia region and over time they came to trust the Phanatic as a civic icon and a valuable asset to a successful performance.

But what would happen if, say, a band was not from the Philadelphia area? What if they weren't Phillies fans? What if a band director had never seen or heard of the Phanatic? Well, I got the chance to answer those questions personally when the Dodgers came calling. Yes, you heard it right, the Los Angeles Dodgers and the hallowed grounds of Chavez Ravine, home of Dodger Blue and noted Phanatic nemesis, Tom Lasorda. In 1982, the Dodgers contacted the Phillies front office and asked if, on the next West Coast trip, they would be willing to bring the Phanatic along so he could entertain the Dodger fans during their pre-game festivities. Bill Giles, of course, thought this sounded like fun. Yes, the Phanatic was coming to Tinsel Town!

I couldn't contain my enthusiasm. All I could focus on was the fact that I would be traveling with the Phillies and going on the road as if I was a member of the team! It was the stuff of my boyhood dreams. I would be traveling to the airport on the team bus and flying to L.A. on the team charter plane. Once in L.A., we would be staying in the team hotel. I didn't for one moment focus on the reality of the Phanatic entertaining in a hostile environment. On the contrary, I imagined the Dodger fans being just like our fans, in love with the Phanatic because he was cute, funny and huggable, but not seeing him as the mascot FOR the Philadelphia Phillies, a hated rival in the National League.

I was really surprised by the reaction of the Phillies players. They were just as excited as I was! I guess it was going to be new for them, too. It must have been kind of like bringing your new puppy over to a friend's house to show him off. "Yeah, Phanatic, we'll take you to L.A. and show you around," they said. "You'll love it because there is no other place like it." Movie stars, gorgeous women and the glitter and glam of Hollywood would be a perfect place for a single guy traveling with superstar professional athletes—or so we all thought. The players' excitement had my mind racing with possibilities about the fun that the Phanatic and I had ahead of us. Of course, it further distracted me from the reality of performing away from the safe and familiar confines of Veterans Stadium instead of the den of the lions that Chavez Ravine would become for the Phillie Phanatic on that day.

From the moment I stepped on the bus to head to the Philly airport, until I got to Dodger Stadium the following evening, it was as exciting as you might imagine. There I was sitting on the charter plane, watching all of the players go through a routine that I suspect they went through hundreds of times before, but I was witnessing it for the first time through the eyes of a huge baseball fan who had just gotten invited to see everything behind the curtain and was now pretending to be just like them. It was an experience and feeling that I still find difficult to describe. Imagine if you were suddenly riding in First Class with your dream job. That was me!

I remember having a drink in the bar that evening after dinner with some of the players. They had a night off before the start of a long West Coast swing. The waitress was someone they knew from their frequent trips to the same L.A. hotel and it was a little like a homecoming of sorts. They were all excited to tell her who I was, and it was apparent she didn't have any idea what they were talking about, so I spent some time trying to explain the Phanatic to her. She was very pretty and I could see after a while that the players were having fun trying to stir up a romance. I appreciated the effort, but after I realized she was a Dodger fan and had absolutely no idea who the Phanatic was, it concerned me. My encounter with the grumpy groundskeeper from Boise happened much later in my career with the Phillies and this was going to be my first experience performing in front of opposing fans. Up to this point, my only work on the road had been in front of friendly audiences in the home ballparks of the Phillies' minor league affiliates. So, I had a bit of a shock when I came to the realization that not only would these Dodger fans not know the Phanatic, but they could very well be hostile. I went to bed that night not feeling as confident as I would otherwise.

The next day, game day, went very quickly. I boarded the bus to Dodger Stadium to a bit of ribbing from players like Larry Bowa who yelled out, "Let's see how many of the f-ing Dodger fans will want to kill the Phanatic tonight!" He told me I had no idea how tough these fans in L.A. can be on them, let alone their goofy, green mascot. I just smiled and let all the other players chime in, including Greg "The Bull" Luzinski, who assured me that when I died in the costume, due to blunt force trauma, I would never be forgotten. LOL.

I was starting to get nervous and when I got to the stadium and carried the Phanatic bag with me into the visiting team locker room, it finally dawned on me where I was. I didn't have to be dressed for at least another three hours. I was, again, distracted by my good fortune and enjoyed that time watching the players get ready for batting and fielding practice. I went out on the field and watched all of the activity that I was used to watching, but only at home. It was fun and relaxing because I was able to watch the fans as they came in and settled into their seats. *They look just like our fans except for the fact that they're wearing Dodger blue*, I said to myself. I looked at my watch and realized that it was time for me to get dressed.

I met with the Dodgers promotions director and he thanked me for coming and said that it was going to be a blast working with the Phanatic. He believed that the Dodgers should have a mascot of their own but knew management would never approve it. Funkillers! He wanted me to do just what I did in Philadelphia during pre-game. I had explained to him previously that the Phanatic's routines were mostly spontaneous. The Phanatic would, however, get involved with any promotion that the Dodgers had planned that night. The Dodgers promotions director responded and told me that there was nothing unusual planned for that night.

"The stage is all yours!" he said.

Great!

But what if I sucked?

Gulp!

Spontaneous performance was not always guaranteed to be great, so at that moment I wished there was some sort of script I could have followed. Larry Bowa's voice was in my head and all I could think of was the Phanatic being set on fire by the Dodgers faithful … with me inside him! I was lucky, however, because donning the Phanatic costume included a transformation of sorts. Once I zipped up that beautiful green fur, David Raymond disappeared and the Phanatic's edgy personality, which included some of that famous Philly swagger, took over. I walked down the tunnel, full of energy and adrenaline, just like my heroes in uniform. I was full of confidence. All of my anxiety was gone. The Phanatic was ready to conquer Dodger Stadium. Bring it on!

I arrived in our dugout. It was about 30 minutes before first pitch and the players were hanging out waiting for the introductions and the national anthem. I was always surprised how loose professional baseball players were before games. I guess it had to do with the length of the baseball season—162 games spread over six months—and the fact that baseball requires mental focus as much as emotion. Many players looked forward to the distraction of the pre-game routine to help them prepare emotionally. A few laughs or an occasional practical joke helped relax the players and built some valuable chemistry. That was the key to the Phanatic's spontaneous interactions with the players. I would seek out the team clown and work directly with him. Crowds always loved to see ball players goof around with the Phanatic. I loved it because it was a challenge for me to crack a player's pre-game focus and get him to react.

When I went to Phillies games as a young boy with my father, I had trouble seeing the players as "real" people. I couldn't relate to them, but every now and then I would catch a glimpse of the players acting "human" and I always remembered it as a thrill to see and made me fond of that particular player. That is why infielder Tony Taylor was one of my favorite players in the late '60s. He had a tremendous personality on the field. He was a ball player, but you always knew there was a human being inside. It was fitting that Tony—a Phillies coach in 1978—was the first person to be photographed with the Phillie Phanatic on the day the green guy debuted.

Anyway, as the Phanatic arrived in the dugout that night in L.A., the players were all jacked up, joking and cheering when they saw him. All at once, they grabbed the Phanatic and pushed him up to the top step of the dugout and shoved him out on to the field. I tripped over the Phanatic's size 30 shoes, purposely fell to the ground then quickly popped up with my arms thrown triumphantly in the air as if to announce my arrival to the stunned Dodger faithful. The crowd responded immediately. It was a small rumble at first but soon became thunder. Yeah, the thunder of 25,000 boos! At first it didn't faze me. But when those boos didn't go away, it became distracting and I had trouble thinking of a way to make them stop.

Instinctually, I went over to the Dodger players because when I was at home, they were my go-to foils. I tried everything. I shook the Phanatic's belly at their dugout. I stuck the 12-inch tongue in Steve Sax's ear. The boos only got louder. Even manager Tommy Lasorda looked like he felt bad for the Phanatic. It would be a few years until the Phanatic's feud with Tommy reached its peak, but at this moment, I thought Tommy might come to the Phanatic's aid. Nope. He turned his back and waddled toward the Dodgers clubhouse, not willing to give me any relief from the punishment of Dodger Stadium.

Feeling desperate and completely unwelcome, I sought my comfort zone. I ran over to the Phillies players where they were warming up along the right field foul line. I started to pretend to play practical jokes on them. They didn't cooperate because they were not used to the Phanatic interacting with them as if they were the visiting team, but also because they enjoyed hearing the Phanatic being pelted with boos. *Better him than us!*

The Phanatic and I were out of answers. We just couldn't create funny distractions to quiet the boos raining down from Dodger Stadium. I had never experienced this before and started to feel defeated. To this day, I remain sympathetic to the players who are pelted with boos after mistakes on the field. I must confess that in my youth I participated in the booing, but now I refrain because of the feeling I experienced that day in Dodger Stadium. Those boos turned the Phanatic into Eeyore and his green, furry shoulders drooped like Winnie the Pooh's forlorn friend. The L.A. fans were winning and I decided that it would be best for me to walk back into the dugout. Maybe I could reboot the Phanatic's true personality and make another entrance, but I was out of ideas and pre-game would be wrapping up in about 15 minutes.

I was ready to give up when I got to the top step of the dugout and looked over the Phanatic's shoulder. Much to my surprise, I saw a high school band marching in single file out to center field! Unbelievable! I felt like I was back in South Philly again. This was perfect and I knew exactly what to do. The Phanatic bolted from the dugout and ran to center field where he met the pretty drum majorette in full stride. I dropped and hugged her feet as if she were royalty (actually she was the Phanatic's savior). I had noticed when I was approaching her that she didn't look afraid and actually had a big, beaming smile on her face. I stepped back from the Phanatic's forced hug to see that smile still beaming and she started to laugh. I laid a big Phanatic Kiss on her face then stumbled backward and pretended to pass out right at her feet. Unfazed and completely focused, she continued to march over the top of the Phanatic's prone body.

Suddenly, I noticed the thunderous booing had stopped and had been replaced with the sounds of applause and laughing. Yes! With the help of that cheerful, laser focused drum majorette, I had distracted them! I had found my West Coast Funster. And she was awesome! This was going to work out after all. The Phanatic stood up and watched the drum majorette and the rest of the band move into formation for their first number. The Phanatic marched over and stood at attention right next to his new friend, the drum majorette. Mimicking her exact body position, the Phanatic turned his head and shot his long tongue at her. The crowd loved it. The sound of laughing was wonderful and it inspired me and the Phanatic, because just a few moments earlier we were ready to walk off the field and give up. Now we were rolling with the spontaneous fun that only the Phanatic could provide.

As the fun picked up, I made my move toward the band but was interrupted by a strong pull on the back of my arm. It almost pulled me off the feet. I turned the Phanatic's head around to see the red, snarling face of the Band Director. He had a death grip on my arm and the Phanatic's wing, screaming, "Get away from my band! You are going to ruin the show!" I was startled at first. I wasn't sure what was happening, but my natural reaction was to yank my arm from his grip. As I did, the Band Director tried to grab back onto the Phanatic's wing but I moved my arm up and all he got was air. When he tried to grab it again, I move it down and again … nothing but air. This impromptu little joust must have looked very comical because I could hear the crowd's laughter intensifying. Man, finally, these fans were responding! I can't tell you how great it is to hear 25,000 fans laughing, clapping and shouting approval. Though I really pissed off the Band Director, I was starting to get the feeling this was going to be a great show, just the kind of entertainment I was hoping to bring to Dodger Stadium.

As I got more confident, I shook off the Band Director and ran toward the band members. I squeezed the Phanatic into their formation and started to weave in and around their lines. Much to my delight the Band Director made chase and continued yelling, "You're ruining our show!! Get off of the field!" One of my most vivid memories of this moment was seeing the faces of the band members as this Muppet Show spontaneously broke out in the middle of their performance. Their faces were filled with pure joy and amuse-ment. FUNSTERS! And as the green guy "tormented" them, they didn't miss a note, a step, or a beat. They were perfect. And they enjoyed the heck out of the Phanatic. I know this because when they lowered their instruments I could see them laughing hysterically and nudging one another. "Look at our Band Director chasing that big, fat, green fury thing!" I could hear them say. If the Phanatic had ears this would have been music to them. At this point, the action in the stands started to become lively. On-field promotions at sporting events are categorized as "value-added entertainment." This kind of entertainment is fun and distracting and usually lightly applauded when finished. But in this case, it was The Show. The fans in Dodger Stadium had become completely captivated by the sight of this large green furball being chased by a red-faced maniac, while a group of high school musicians played flawlessly.

I was quickly becoming winded during that chase on the Dodger Stadium field. Running is one of the hardest and most physically demanding tasks to perform while in costume. And I mean almost any distance. Unless you have performed in costume, you can't imagine just how hard it is. I was physically shot and realized it was time for a break. I had put a little bit of distance between the Phanatic and the red-faced Band Director and saw my opportunity to get back to the safety of the Phillies clubhouse through the right field tunnel. I had completely turned the crowd around—from jeering to cheering—with a surprise "invasion" of an innocent pre-game event. Instead of booing, the crowd cheered wildly as the Band Director chased the Phanatic. Half of them were just enjoying the show, while the other half wanted the Band Director to catch and dismember the Phanatic. Well, I wasn't going to give him that chance. My pre-game job was done here, so I broke from the band and ran toward right field.

Suddenly, a horrific sight stopped me dead in my tracks. Thirty yards from me were two gigantic L.A. police officers—and they were sprinting directly toward the Phanatic! The guy inside the costume—*me!*—was terrified. These guys were motorcycle cops, you know, CHIP officers with the bike helmets and chin straps pulled so tight that it plastered a nasty snarl on their faces. It felt like

I was watching in slow motion as their holstered guns and shiny handcuffs bounced up and down on their hips. The Phanatic was frozen in place as if he'd been turned to stone. The guy inside the costume was petrified as well. All I could think about was being thrown in an L.A. jail, dressed as a freaking Muppet, and never seeing the light of day. I was, after all, an enemy of the state!

As I stood frozen, staring at those two L.A. cops, the Band Director caught up to me and grabbed the Phanatic's wing. "Get him off of the field!" the red-face Funkiller shouted. "He's ruining the show!" He had made a citizen's arrest and was thrilled to have reinforcements. As the officers moved in, I braced for the inevitable command to "assume the position" and to be handcuffed to the glee of 25,000 Dodger fans. But as I braced the Phanatic's body for a clash, something stunning happened—the cops ran right by the Phanatic, grabbed the Band Director and dragged him off of the field!

As the police dragged the red-faced Funkiller off, I stood in frozen amazement until the crowd's reaction shook me from that state. The band was starting to file off of the field and it was receiving a standing ovation from the Dodger faithful. I was elated that the crowd gave those kids that well-deserved show of appreciation for not being distracted in any way by the Muppet Show that had broken out in the middle of their performance. They were fantastic. As they marched off the field the Phanatic dropped to his knees, extended his hands, and bowed up and down in heartfelt, "I'm not worthy" tribute.

I have never forgotten those faces. Ear to ear smiles and wonderful looks of disbelief and accomplishment. The Phanatic and I marched in mock stride behind the band and off the field. They went their way and I went mine—straight to the visiting clubhouse. I shed my costume and the Phanatic's personality began to melt away. The locker room was deserted except for some of the clubhouse personnel and none of them had seen the pre-game show. All of the players and coaches were in the dugout or on the field, so I couldn't get their reaction to what had just happened. I was exhausted, so I just sat and reflected on the performance. After a few minutes, I began to feel bad for the Band Director—after all, he was just trying to protect his students. I was curious to know if he had indeed been escorted off to jail. I really hoped that wasn't the case.

I decided to go check on the Band Director. I threw on my warmups and my Phillies cap and ran out to try and find him. I was surprised to find him pretty quickly in an auxiliary locker room. I went over and tapped him on the shoulder. He turned and looked at me.

"Hi! I'm the person that was in the Phanatic costume," I said.

I had wanted to apologize to him for not asking for permission to work with his band.

He stopped me.

"Please don't apologize," he said. "I had no idea that you were a professional. I had no idea you were approved by the Dodgers to be on the field. I actually thought you were some crazed Philadelphia fan that had run out of the stands!"

I was completely floored by his response. I thought he was going to be pissed. I thought he was going to read me the riot act. I thought he was going to recite the Battle Cry of the Funkiller word for word. Instead he expressed his gratitude for the Phanatic taking part in his band's performance!

He actually called me a professional!

A professional?

A professional idiot, he should have said—and he would have been completely correct. I WAS a crazed Philadelphia fan and I did have the Dodgers' approval to be on the field. But I will always love how the Band Director called me a Professional idiot that night and I have been introducing myself as such ever since.

The Band Director went on to thank me for helping his band receive its first ever standing ovation at Dodger Stadium. It never would have happened without the Phanatic intervening. I told him that our "chase" enhanced the show and we should be proud. He laughed and we shook hands and all was right with the world! I wish things had ended as well with grumpy Joe in Boise.

As the dust settled on my Dodger Stadium adventure, I began to reflect on those folks I call Funkillers.

What are they?

Are they just cranky, ill-tempered people who simply can't stand anyone around them having fun?

Or are they just following their instincts, trying to keep us Funsters safe and on track?

Over the years, as the Power of Fun has evolved inside of me, I have answered these questions differently. For most of my years with the Phillies, I would attach the label of Funkiller to anyone who wouldn't cooperate and laugh at the Phanatic's antics. Senator Ted Kennedy and Cal Ripken Sr., come to mind as especially infamous Funkillers. They took themselves way too seriously and refused to play along when they had encounters with the Phanatic. Way more often than not, however, the Phanatic received overwhelmingly positive feedback all over the country. Still, I found it frustrating when the occasional Funkiller would surface with a scowl and tell the Phanatic to buzz off. Thank goodness they were few and far between.

On the rare occasions when I did encounter a Funkiller, I tried not to let him frustrate me too much. Instead, the Phanatic and I tried to use the Funkiller's negative vibe as a positive, as a challenge, and we would do our best to wrestle a smile out of the Funkiller. But all these years later, when I look back and consider the perspective of the Funkillers, I recognize that they were simply acting natural. They had been programmed to look for potential problems and danger and avert those situations at all costs. Even though I remain staunchly committed to my Funster principles, I now understand where the Funkillers were coming from. My view of them, you could say, has evolved—just like that Band Director's view of me and the Phanatic did all those years ago in Los Angeles.

Today, if you asked my friend the Band Director if he'd be willing to endure a few comic interruptions to his band's perfor-mance in return for his students receiving a standing ovation at Dodger Stadium, he'd say, "Hell, yeah." He might have played a classic Funkiller's role as he chased the Phanatic all over the field that long-ago night. Hey, he was instinctually trying to protect his students from failure and embarrassment, and I understand that now. But when he saw those smiles on his students' faces and heard the cheers from the stands, he became a believer, just another convert to the Power of Fun.

Lesson Three: N.
"No!"

Let's look at some of the iconic Funkillers to better understand why they respond the way they do and recognize how they can become a valuable tool in creating powerful fun. Imagine all of the editing power our parents, coaches and teachers had over us as we were growing up. Let's consider that these folks are talented in their leadership position and are not abusive in any way. What did we think of them then? How do we remember their guidance and support now? Has our perspective changed at all while we have assumed some of those roles in our own lives today?

In Malcolm Gladwell's book *David and Goliath*, he discusses his theory of "desirable difficulty." He presents a powerful case that the lives of extraordinary successful people were made possible, in part, due to the extreme life challenges that they were presented with at an early age. The loss of either or both parents, dyslexia and other serious struggles, if overcome, provided people like Brian Grazer, one of the most successful Hollywood producers of all time, with unique combinations of perspective and skill that helped him excel.

One of the most compelling profiles in Gladwell's chapter about desirable difficulty was of Dr. Emil J. Freireich. He was a child of the Great Depression whose father died suddenly when he was very young. He lived in a small apartment in Humboldt Park, in Chicago, that bordered a ghetto. After his father's death, his mother had to go work in a sweat shop and was never home. The only "mother" he had growing up was an Irish immigrant woman his mother hired to watch him. The Irish woman was out of work and needed the money for her rent. It was, by all accounts, a life that would not breed success, yet Jay Freireich grew up to be a Doctor of Oncology at the National Cancer Institute in 1955, and went on to be credited for developing advances in chemotherapy that have led to curing thousands and thousands of children stricken with leukemia. One of his best assets or "skills" that Gladwell points out as a product of his difficult upbringing was his lack of fear to go against virtually all of the conventional thinking of his day with regards to childhood leukemia treatments. He was zealous in his pursuits and never doubted what he was doing would lead to success. A person that possessed a normal resistance to fear would not have accomplished what he did.

The Battle Cry of the Funkiller is driven by fear. Our parents don't want us to be hurt, so they do their best to protect us from danger. Our leaders want to see us become successful, but they are fearful of going against conventional wisdom to reach our goals. The Funkiller's advice, in most cases, is given from a very educated and successful perspective. They most likely have experienced success by risking it all and taking great chances, but directing others to do the same seems too risky for them to advise. Brian Grazer, made stronger by overcoming dyslexia, developed a unique negotiating skill that in part made him the most successful movie producer in Hollywood, but when asked if he would wish dyslexia on his children his answer was a resounding, "No!" Isn't that the battle cry of a Funkiller? How do we take the passionate cry for protecting those that we care about without extinguishing their ability to grow and enjoy the Power of Fun?

We need to bring the Funkillers in and ask them for help. Their special vision and expertise can help us be safe and appropriate while we create, build and execute our own Power of Fun Plan™. The pursuit of powerful fun will not be successful unless we make sure we are being safe and cautious as we design our fun. Once the Funkiller is a member of our group being asked to help pave a path toward powerful fun, they become invested in our success.

They want us to succeed and take measured risks while negotiating the "politically correct" barriers we are confronted with today. This process will remove the Funkiller from a role of "leadership oversight" and make them a valuable member of our creative team dedicated to the development of powerful fun. This will turn the Funkillers' "No" into a resounding "Yes!"

I have the wonderful opportunity to present the Power of Fun story to hundreds of groups all over the country. My audiences range from corporate leadership to boots-on-the-ground employees. I even have had the pleasure of speaking to thousands of high school students from around the country that have done well in school and were invited to come to the Freedoms Foundation campus in Valley Forge, Pennsylvania. Everyone always enjoys the Funkiller stories. The "Battle Cry of the Funkiller" is highlighted in a video called "Never Failed" and does a fantastic job of illustrating the damage that can be done by a Funkiller unopposed. During early reviews in Lucille Ball's career, she was told she was "too shy" to be successful as a performer! The Decca Recording Company turned down the Beatles because they didn't like their sound and guitar music was on the way out. Decca instead signed Brian Poole and the Tremeloes and today is considered one of the biggest mistakes in music history! I loved to hear the story about how the Funkillers at The Kansas City Star fired Walt Disney because his artwork "lacked imagination" and contained no "original ideas"!

If we are going to invest in the first two lessons in the development of Powerful Fun, we have to recognize the danger in rolling out anything unexpected or creative without some editing. The "Battle Cry of the Funkiller" is the desire of those who want to protect us from harm. By being inclusive during our creative process and purposely adding a negative voice in the room, we will create Serious Fun. Fun that has been planned, developed, created, rehearsed, vetted and edited will be endorsed by even the most diffi-cult critic or actuary. By understanding their motivation and using their guidance, we can avoid mistakes that would stop our pursuit of Powerful Fun. We can make our Funkillers invested partners in our development of Serious Fun. We must be relentless and fearless in our belief that fun starts with that simple choice, but ultimately it will not be Powerful Fun unless it becomes Serious Fun.

CHAPTER 4

The Power of Distracting Fun

"Your mother has eight months to live.
Have a nice day."

– My mom's doctor

Unfortunately, life can be hard. In fact, it can be brutal. I have experienced that brutality and it would have consumed me if not for the beauty and the power hidden in that green, furry shag carpet.

The Phanatic's personality literally saved my life!

In 1989, my mom was diagnosed with a grade 4 glioblastoma brain tumor and was given only eight months to live. She was just 59.

Growing up, my life was idyllic. Looking back now, I truly lived a dream. My family was respected, we were healthy and we lived in a typical middle-class neighborhood with plenty of kids our age to run with. I played sports and did well in school. I cannot remember any time as a kid where I was depressed, scared or challenged in any way.

Well, I guess there was that time when I was eight or nine and was heading down to the park behind our house to play. I was running down a grassy hill and slipped and fell on a mud wasp nest. Those nasty wasps, clearly not happy with their 90-pound intruder, went into attack mode and swarmed me. I remember screaming and swatting at the wasps as they stung my head and face. I ended up with a trip to the hospital and over 90 stings.

As I was being attacked that day, a woman from another house adjacent to the park saw me in distress and realized what was happening. She came running out with a broom and commenced with a beating that was meant for the wasps but mostly added additional pain and stress to me.

Back at our house, my mom had stayed in the front yard to watch me get safely to the park entrance. Our front porch was at least 200 yards away, and from Mom's vantage point, all she could see was some crazed neighbor violently attacking her youngest with a broom. She immediately bolted into action and ran those 200 yards faster than an Olympic sprinter to come to my rescue. It must have been a hysterical sight if you were just passing by. Mom caught the broom-wielding neighbor mid-swing, yanked "the weapon" from her grasp and was about to take a mighty swing of her own when she finally realized what was happening. Mom didn't have time to be embarrassed because I was still under attack. She held on to that broom and helped me survive that wasp attack. This remains a funny and wonderful memory because it reminds me how much Mom loved us, and the lengths she'd go to protect us.

I wish I could have protected her from cancer some 25 years later.

I remember the first time I thought something wasn't right with Mom. We were longtime members of Newark Country Club and during my years as the Phanatic, golf was my passion. I loved playing in the early afternoons before I'd go to an appearance or the Vet for a game. Usually I would play a quick nine holes alone and work on my game. It was my only competitive outlet since graduating from college and it was great for me mentally and physically, because I always walked and carried a bag. One day, I was coming up the fairway on the par-5 15th hole, when I noticed a group of women just finishing up. As I finished the hole and started toward the 16th tee, I looked up and saw the women waiting to let me play through. My mom was in the group. It was one of those fleeting moments in life, one that is usually forgotten quickly. This one, however, stayed with me and became seared in my brain because it was a troubling harbinger of things to come.

I gave Mom a little kiss on the cheek and thanked her and the group for allowing me to play through. But as I walked down the 16th fairway that day, it occurred to me that my mom didn't look well. It wasn't anything specific. It may have been her color or eyes that somehow didn't look right to me. I passed it off as her being tired from the golf. I told my dad about it later and he said that she had come home complaining of a stiff neck and a little dizziness. It wasn't a big deal at the time and he was going to take her in to see the training staff at the University of Delaware to get some treatment. It was late July and Dad was gearing up for preseason football training camp. A few days later, Dad called. He was concerned because Mom hadn't responded to the treatment. She continued to experience dizziness and was in discomfort. There was concern that it was a return of her Meniere's disease.

Mom had contracted Meniere's disease—a disease of the inner ear that causes hearing loss and vertigo—when I was 3 and it took her hearing when she was 29. Ironically, my mom's being deaf was one of the reasons I naturally developed some of those nonverbal communication skills that served me so well as a physical performer in costume. Several years into my career as the Phanatic, I was asked by a reporter if growing up with a deaf mother led to my physical and nonverbal performance success? I wasn't sure how to answer that question, so I asked Mom and she reminded me how animated I would get when she would discipline me in my teenager years. As I would start to protest whatever punishment she imposed, she would just turn off her hearing aid and walk away. My nonverbal responses in those instances were classic Phillie Phanatic moves, she told me.

Mom turned her "handicap" into a career of service to the deaf community in Delaware. She worked as a counselor at Sterk School for the Deaf and became a certified interpreter. She was named Deaf Woman of the Year in Delaware in 1979. She was a very special woman, raised in an "old school" time where women stayed home and provided for their families. After the kids had grown, she became somewhat of a renaissance woman. She had great talents. Her greatest might have been her ability to build a meaningful career out of a life challenge that would have discouraged many others. It is an understatement to say I was proud of her—I still am—and that pride can be shared by Phillie Phanatic fans everywhere because she definitely had a role in developing the big, green guy's personality.

The athletic trainers at UD suggested that my dad schedule an MRI for Mom, just to rule out anything major. Dad had a schedule conflict and asked if I could get her to and from the appointment. He said it was just routine and that we'd get to the bottom of what was causing her struggles and fix it. Unfortunately, that would not become an option. I took her to that appointment and got her safely back home. It was uneventful and she even looked a bit better to me, though she usually was not one to complain to her youngest son. I dropped her off at home and didn't give it much more thought. I was in the middle of the baseball season and had an enormous amount of work to do and I was confident that all would be OK. That confidence was the result of living an idyllic life.

The next thing I remember was my dad calling about two weeks later and asking me to join Mom and him, along with my sister and brother, at a doctor's office in Wilmington. They had discovered the problem and wanted to talk to us about how we could help with her treatment. That was good news, I thought. I was glad the results were in and we could be helpful in getting her back on her feet. I really had no idea where this was headed and was completely blindsided by the news to come.

We met the following day in the office of a doctor I had never heard of. He was the kind of doctor I never even knew existed. It felt strange. We were ushered into an office, not an examination room. The doctor sat behind a desk. Mom and Dad sat to my right. My older brother Chris and sister Debbie were behind me. The mood, at first, was not really somber. But moments after we sat down, I felt a shot of fear run down my back. I hadn't been completely focused as the meeting began. It was just another part of my busy day. I wasn't expecting any bad news, and for the first time, I realized this could be bad news we were about to hear. My heart started to race. I focused on the doctor's lips and mouth as he started to speak. He spoke in a soft monotone voice. He was saying that after viewing Mom's MRI, it was confirmed that there was a large, malignant tumor in her brain. It was a stage 4 glioblastoma and even though it was operable, there wasn't hope for long-term survival. In his estimation, Mom had eight months to live—and that was if the treatment went well. In short, Mom was dying.

It took a few minutes for all this to sink in—and at least three months before I recognized how angry I was at this doctor. I learned much later that he didn't believe in dispensing "false hope" and felt it important to be brutally honest with his patients. Meanwhile, Mom hadn't been his patient for much longer than 24 hours and he decided it was important to plant the notion in her head that her life would be over in eight months. My mom was raised to believe that doctors were from a higher order and what they said was gospel. They were to be listened to and not questioned. Her doctor told her that day she had eight months to live and that was that.

I couldn't stay in the office any longer. Mom and Dad were discussing the details with the doctor as if they were getting directions to the mall. I was sweating and felt confused and dizzy. I walked out of his office, headed down the hall and out the back of the building to the sidewalk. I walked a few blocks and distinctly remember thinking how beautiful a day it was. Then, all the emotion hit me at once. I stopped, sat down at the base of a big oak tree and broke down. It was so strange to feel that type of grief. My life to that point included no real challenges and now I had to face one like this. I was scared for my mom and what was ahead for her, but at the same time petrified over how I could possibly deal with her suffering and death. The tears felt good because they seemed to be natural, but fear was not something that I would have expected. Over the next eight months, I discovered so many unexpected emotions that come with watching someone close to you die. My life to that point was a Hollywood script that included little experience with tragedy. I don't remember friends of mine, even though I am sure it happened, going through this type of tragedy. Our family would be tested soon with the unexpected feelings of guilt, selfishness and pain that roll over you like an unstoppable force that you cannot avoid.

Over the next few weeks, we came together and supported Mom through her surgery and treatments. She was only in the hospital for four days before she came home. We eventually had to use hospice care during the last month of her life. The most difficult time for me was when I would try and comprehend what my mom was going through and the fear she must have been experiencing. What was it like when she would wake up in the middle of the night and know she was going to die? How lonely and scary that must have been for her. There was no way Dad or any of us could shield her from those fears and that was difficult.

Mom, or Suzie, as Dad always called her, passed away peacefully and quietly at home in the spring of 1990, almost eight months to the day of her diagnosis. I tried, with all the courage I could muster, to testify at her memorial service in the same Newark Methodist Church where she had encouraged me to become an acolyte, but I broke down just minutes after I started speaking. I was so embarrassed that I couldn't stand up for her when it was my turn. Everyone else had done such a beautiful job. Thankfully, Father Jim Dever, my friend and as close to a spiritual advisor I have ever had, came to my support in a quiet moment in the back of the church after Mom's service had ended. He said, "David, you were perfect. Up to that point, everyone was composed and flawless. But this moment called for emotion. You provided that emotional component and it was important to your mom's service. After you spoke, everyone was given permission to cry. I am sure your mother is proud."

Father Dever should have been a coach! I guess, in a way, that is what he really is.

The next few weeks were a blur and as Mother's Day approached,

I decided to go on a golfing trip with Dad and couple of his buddies from Newark Country Club. I felt like it was the perfect opportunity to get away, to forget about this Mother's Day because Mom wasn't there, and spend some quality time with my dad before football became his distraction.

I never thought about this trip from my wife's perspective. She would be home alone with our 6-month-old son Kyle. It never occurred to me that this was *her* first Mother's Day. I failed to think about my absence from her perspective. I failed to think about how the eight-month ordeal of my mom's cancer affected our marriage. During my many visits with Mom while she was sick, she reminded me to focus on my family and make sure I was not forgetting about being a father and husband. I failed to listen and believed everything was all right in my home and my marriage. I hadn't been paying attention.

The golfing trip proved to be a Godsend for dad and me. We always had a complicated relationship because he was my father and my coach, but after I had graduated from Delaware, I found us growing closer. Golf was now our connector. We had fun and for a few days the misery and sadness of Mom's suffering and passing dimmed a bit. I was looking forward to getting home and spending time with my family. My young son Kyle was growing and changing each day. I believe my mom used his birth date as a goal to stay with us so she could witness his arrival. She reached that goal and her words to me about the importance of seeing my children grow and being a good father were in my mind as I walked in the front door from the golf trip.

No one was home so I dumped my bag in the bedroom and walked out to the kitchen to see if there was a note from my wife letting me know where she and Kyle were. There was a note, but not the kind I was expecting or hoping for. Instead, it was a long letter from Christine telling me she had decided to leave and take Kyle with her. They would be staying with her mom in Philadelphia until she found another place to live.

There is much complexity to the dissolution of a marriage. With the benefit of hindsight, there were many warning signs that my marriage was in trouble, but in the moment, I was blindsided. The confusion and almost surreal fog in my mind were the least of my struggles. I remember collapsing on the kitchen floor knowing with certainty that I would not survive, because the weight of my mom's passing followed by my family being torn apart was unbearable. I felt completely alone and void of any thought about whom I could seek out for comfort. In one short moment, I had lost faith in my ability to trust my decisions or actions. Suddenly, putting one foot in front of the other seemed impossible, let alone doing my job— which was to be a freaking clown!

In a span of three weeks, I buried my mom and began the process of navigating a separation and divorce. This also happened to be the busiest time for my work, the start of my 12th season working for the Phillies. The Phillies were very supportive during this tough time and they offered to clear some of my schedule. I missed only four games in 16 years and two of them were for my mom's memorial services. So many members of my Phillies family were there to say goodbye to Mom. I'm not sure why, but I declined their offers to cancel appearances. Instead, on the day after I collapsed at home after reading that heartbreaking letter from Christine, I decided to honor a commitment and make a two-hour Phanatic appearance in King of Prussia.

I remember dragging myself to that appearance. I felt like I was moving in slow motion, pulling each piece of the Phanatic costume slowly out of the bag and dropping it on the floor. Shoes, legs, body, head and jersey. Every piece felt like it was 1,000 pounds. The Phanatic was now just an empty heap of green fur on the floor. He looked like I felt—empty and sad with no life or energy. Little did I know, however, that something amazing was about to happen that day.

As I sluggishly zipped the Phanatic's body around me and pulled his head over mine, I felt his powerful personality suddenly take over. You know when you read about people recounting an "out of body" experience? Well, that was happening to me. Literally. I was there, but the Phanatic's personality was in charge. The grief and sorrow I was experiencing completely disappeared. It was as if my reality was floating out of focus in the background while the Phanatic entertained both the crowd and me! For all of those years, I was the guy leading the Phanatic. On that difficult day, he led me. For the next few months, the Phanatic's personality became my refuge and I was given some much-needed time to regain focus and meaning in my life.

For me, the beauty and power of that green fur represented the most valuable lesson in the Power of Fun: The Power of Distracting Fun. The Phanatic's personality saved me in 1990, and helped me recognize how important it was to *choose* fun, especially when life became brutal. This lesson helped me crawl out of a deep hole of depression after the loss of my mom and the breakup of my marriage. Eventually, the lesson helped me trust again and that trust led me to a beautiful relationship—27 years and counting!—with my wife Sandy and the creation of Kyle's sisters and brother. Maddie, Carly and Dylan are here, in no small part, because of the Power of Distracting Fun.

You might not have the Phanatic's personality living inside you like I did, but you do have the power to choose the distraction of fun when life's brutality visits you. It may sound counterintuitive, but your own intentional activities will distract and save you! And I don't care what those intentional activities are. It could be a quiet walk or meditation. It could be doing a puzzle or just getting together with that friend that always makes you smile. These intentional activities, regardless of what they are, will re-wire your brain, refresh your perspective and give you the energy and power to get back to life during the most difficult of times.

Sinister Brain Wiring

It took me years to really understand why the Phanatic, or mascots in general, are so powerful. I have been asked that question many, many times over the years and all those questions have helped me arrive at my answer.

Mascots use fun as a tool to grab and distract us. Once an audience is distracted, it can build an emotional connection with the mascot. When there is an emotional connection between the two, a strong, positive and lasting relationship is created. From a marketing perspective, an emotional connection to the customer is the ideal end game and will drive long-term revenue. From a life perspective, an emotional connection can create the ability to heal emotional and physical wounds. As the Phanatic, I have seen it work thousands of times during my performances, and I have experienced that power personally. Mascots use the Power of Fun to help reprogram our negative brains and you can too. Our negative brains are the problem.

I have been delivering my Powerful Fun keynote for over 20 years and once folks in attendance see the simplicity of the first three lessons of the F.U.N. of fun, some become a little skeptical. Come on. *Life can be difficult. I can't just choose fun.*

Oh, yes, you can—if you can overcome the negative brain wiring that prevents you from choosing fun as a tool to survive difficult times and, ultimately, thrive in good times. The "Negative Brain Bias" is the culprit in all of this and it has been studied extensively.

Our negative brain bias has been "hard-wired" into our brains over millions of years of evolution. We don't need it for survival like we needed it way back when, but it is always there, slowly picking away at our ability to focus on the positive. In a very real sense, we are tuned into negative stimuli even though we don't realize it. This is why painful mental and physical experiences remain seared into our brains and are easy to recount, with detail, years later. It's the same reason why the billion-dollar news industry starts every broadcast with adjectives like "devastating" or "catastrophic." Our brains are just built to be sensitive to bad news.

Read this excerpt from a *Psychology Today* article about a study done on our negative brain bias.

> *"Research done by John Cacioppo, Ph.D., included showing people pictures known to arouse positive feelings (say, a Ferrari, or a pizza), those certain to stir up negative feelings (a mutilated face or dead cat) and those known to produce neutral feelings (a plate, a hair dryer). Meanwhile, he recorded electrical activity in the brain's cerebral cortex that reflects the magnitude of information processing taking place.*
>
> *The brain, Cacioppo demonstrated, reacts more strongly to stimuli it deems negative. There is a greater surge in electrical activity. Thus, our attitudes are more heavily influenced by downbeat news than good news."*

You can perform your own "unscientific" research just like I have been doing for years with my audiences. Grab a stopwatch and ask someone this simple question: "Can you tell me something good?" Start the stopwatch as soon as you finish asking the question and stop it once they give an answer. Note the time then ask this second simple question: "What do you hate?" Again, start the stopwatch when you are done asking the question and stop it when they give you an answer. In most cases, the time between the question and the answer will be significantly longer when a positive response is sought.

I love performing this test live because watching people search for a definitively positive response to the "Tell Me Something Good" question is entertaining. They pause, audibly at times, with an "ahhhhh," but their nonverbal reaction is very interesting. They shift from one foot to the other. Sometimes they lean away from me and contort their faces in funny ways. Then, when they come up with an answer, they smile broadly and look proud of themselves. I look at these responses as the physical reflection of the negative brain bias.

So, now that we know what we are up against, how do we combat this sinister brain wiring? The good news is that it's pretty easy!

Did you know that 40 percent of your mood right now is totally up to you? That's right. Almost half of your mood during each second of your life is up to you. This is all due to your intentional activities. So when you wake up in the morning, decide to be happy and your mood will be lifted in a positive way. 50 percent of your mood is shaped by a combination of your negative brain bias and your DNA. 10 percent is determined by what your life circumstances are at any particular time. So take control of that other 40 percent. Decide to be happy.

Here's some more good news: If you practice intentional activities to be happy each day, you can overcome the negative brain bias and even rewire your brain. You can learn to be in charge of up to 80 percent of your mood! Double that 40 percent! This is by no means easy to accomplish or master. It takes time, discipline and hard work. Remember, our effort in using the Power of Fun to be happier, healthier and more productive is Serious Fun and it isn't always easy. Factors like the negative brain bias, our DNA and life circumstances will always fight against us and we will occasionally encounter difficult times. Practicing intentional positive activities will be our ammunition against those negative forces.

Imagine if happiness was a skill set that could be attained through practice. Well, actually, it is! Look at what Dr. Lori Santos is teaching students at Yale University these days. The class is called the *Psychology and the Good Life* or *How to be Happy* and the student engagement has been awesome. It has quickly become the most popular undergraduate course at Yale. Ever!

Students are required to do "Happiness Homework" that includes getting eight hours of sleep, doing something kind for someone and writing down five things they are grateful for. Students find it hard to correct old habits and detach from smart phones and social media. But once they give it a try, they find that after some focus, they indeed feel better.

Dr. Santos believes that if her students sincerely commit to this study, they can change their culture in a big way. But you don't have to go to Yale to learn to take these simple steps to engage with the Power of Fun. How you deal with your mood is up to you. Happiness IS a skill set that can be attained through practice! The question is, will you be a world-class practitioner of Fun or just an amateur?

Lesson 4: Distracting Fun

Successfully using the Power of Fun in life requires understanding that it is OK to be sad. I have been delivering my theory of Powerful Fun for over 20 years and once folks hear the simplicity of the first three lessons, some become skeptical. "Life can be difficult," they say. "It can't be that simple to just choose fun." It's true that there will be difficult times in your life and there is some serious negative brain wiring trying to keep us focused on the negative. But if we practice choosing fun despite all that, we can use fun as a tool to survive those difficult times and thrive during the good ones. You can succeed in adding Powerful Fun to your life. Just make the choice.

CHAPTER 5
Schmitty Validates Fun

"You're trying your damnedest,
you strike out, and they boo you."
– Mike Schmidt, Philadelphia legend,
Major League Baseball Hall of Famer

When discussing the greatest athletes who have ever played in the city of Philadelphia, you will most assuredly want to include Mike Schmidt on that Top 10 list.

We certainly have been treated to some great athletes over the last century in the city of Brotherly Love. When you think about that list, nicknames come to mind:

Concrete Charlie – Chuck Bednarik.

Lefty – Steve Carlton.

Wilt the Stilt – Wilt Chamberlain.

The Round Mound of Rebound – Charles Barkley.

But for Mike Schmidt, there was no catchy nickname. That type of honor seemed to be reserved for our most beloved athletes, and Schmidt, for most of his career, did not qualify as beloved. He was arguably the greatest third baseman to ever play the game, yet for the majority of his career—one played entirely in Philadelphia—he was not appreciated, and in some cases, was even despised by the Phillies faithful.

How could this happen?

Glen Macnow, a longtime Philadelphia sports writer and radio talk show host, seemed to capture the essence of the Philadelphia fan base when he was quoted in a 1995 article about Mike and his relationship with the fans.

Macnow said, "This isn't so much a sports town as a hardware store. When it comes to sports, we are strictly row homes and lunch pails, clock-punchers and blue collars. We demand our heroes to be gritty and rumpled, perhaps with a broken nose and a little dried blood caked under the fingernails."

That would not be the way Macnow, or anyone else who watched the Phillies play, would describe Mike Schmidt. Mike was the antithesis of that. He worked the hot corner with grace and ease. Rarely do I remember seeing his uniform dirty. He was so talented that many times his great plays seemed at first pedestrian. Then you'd see the replay, shake your head and ask your buddy if that really just happened.

Philadelphia fans love emotion in their players. But Mike could be stoic, even a little aloof. He found it difficult to demonstrate emotion outwardly, at least until that tearful day, in 1989, when he announced his retirement while playing on the road in San Diego. The blue collars of this town were always slow to embrace and understand Mike. I think, in many respects, they always hoped to see another side of him, a side that wasn't always smooth and cool. Sadly, it appeared that relationship would never develop—until one July evening late in Mike's career when the Power of Fun intervened and helped him receive a big show of affection and appreciation that continues today.

This connection between Mike and Philadelphia Phillies fans started out in an odd way. In fact, back in June 1985, it appeared that Mike would be run right out of town by angry fans carrying pitchforks! Schmidt was moving toward retirement back then. His ailing knees had forced a move to first base. He was also going through a very difficult slump hitting just .237 with 9 home runs and 32 RBIs. Nightly, he was suffering the wrath of the famous Philly boo birds.

During a trip to Montreal, Schmidt did an interview with a Canadian reporter. He went off on the Philadelphia fans, calling them "a mob scene." He said they were "beyond hope." He added, "I'll tell you something about my playing career in Philadelphia. Whatever I've got in my career now, I would have had a great deal more if I had played my whole career in Los Angeles or Chicago—you name a town—somewhere where they were just grateful to have me around."

Maybe Schmidt thought his comments would not make it across the border, but they did—and they were not received well by the fans, to say the least! I remember reading the article and exclaiming, out loud, "Oh, my God, this isn't going to be pretty!" I turned on sports talk radio and the reaction was coming fast and furious. And it was angry. Ticked-off fans flocked to the ticket windows to buy tickets for the Phillies' first game back at the Vet later in the week. They couldn't wait to get Mike Schmidt. It was going to be the biggest "boo-fest" in Philadelphia sports history.

"This is not going to be pretty," Larry Shenk, the Phillies director of public relations, said.

Shenk went into full damage control. The national media loved every opportunity it got to shine a negative light on Philadelphia fans. The organization feared this was going to be an unwanted spectacle. It was going to be a circus and everyone, including the entire front office, was anxious about what might happen. I'm sure that Schmidt, upon reflection, regretted blowing off some steam in the fans' direction during that interview in Montreal, but it was done, and I assume he was resigned to the fact that he was going to face a very volatile reaction during his first game back at the Vet. And knowing him, I'm sure he was even a little curious to see what the reaction would be.

Don't let any professional athlete tell you that it isn't unnerving to be the target of anger, boos and obscenities hurled down from the stands by 25,000 or more people. Mike, in fact, confirmed this when he said: "You're trying your damnedest, you strike out and they boo you. I act like it doesn't bother me, like I don't hear anything the fans say, but the truth is, I hear every word of it and it kills me."

On that night back at the Vet after the trip to Montreal, Mike's teammates had some fun at his expense. In the clubhouse, they tried to ease his fear before the verbal assault he was soon to receive. They joked about letting him go out on the field alone during introductions. Pitcher Larry Andersen, the class clown of that team, went a step further and suggested that Mike beat the fans to the punch and have some fun with the moment. I can still see what happened next.

I had just finished my pre-game routine as the Phanatic and was getting ready to stand with the umpires and the Phillies ball girls for the National Anthem. Like everyone else in the ballpark, I was filled with anticipation for the introductions of the Phillies players as they took the field. It was the moment when the fans would have their response to Mike Schmidt and things he said in Montreal. Was it going to be as ugly and mean as everyone thought?

"Here are your Philadelphia Phillies!" public address man Dan Baker told the crowd.

The Phillies started to spill out of the dugout, first the outfielders followed by the middle infield and then finally Mike Schmidt jogging out to first base.

Through the green fur, I watched and listened to it all. The first thing I noticed was the immediate guttural sound of boos. They started slowly and began to build toward a crescendo. Then they suddenly stopped! Like everyone else in the stadium that day, I took a look at Mike. Then I took a second look at Mike because something was different. There he was, standing at first base, throwing grounders to the infield wearing a long, red wig and dark sunglasses. I couldn't believe it! He had taken the field in mock disguise. It was so wonderful to see him let his hair down (pardon the pun) and poke fun at his comments and the stress it had produced for the Phillies faithful. There I was, dressed as the Phanatic, trying to stay in character, but at the same time becoming a Super Fan of Mike Schmidt on the spot. I couldn't contain my enthusiasm watching that transformation. The crowd at the Vet experienced the same feeling. The booing stopped and they gave Mike Schmidt a standing ovation.

The anger had been replaced by amusement. It was unbelievable.

I believe this was how the fans wanted to treat Mike all along and it finally happened because Larry Andersen convinced him that fun would be his powerful ally. Just like Bill Giles, Larry was a natural Funster. It was part of his fiber. He couldn't see life in any other way. There was always a place for fun regardless of how others around him felt about it. It is also one of the reasons that Larry is now a beloved color commentator on the team's broadcast crew, following in the footsteps of another Funster, Richie Ashburn. Larry knew that convincing Mike to wear a wig and sunglasses for that difficult moment would put the fans in a better mood. It was a perfect dose of distracting fun—and the greatest third baseman ever temporarily became a distraction therapist practicing distraction therapy.

Today, Michael Jack Schmidt, as he is affectionately referred to, is greatly appreciated for all that he brought to the game of baseball and the Phillies organization. He is on all of our Top 10 lists of beloved superstars in part because he invested in the Power of Fun. For the record, he went 2 for 5 that day in a loss to the Cubs. Even Fun can't make you hit .500 or win every game, but it can sure defuse a difficult situation.

CHAPTER 6
A Trip to the Galapagos

"David, they thrive because they selected
the gene for play!"

– Celso Montalvo, Galapagos Naturalist

Even more validation for the Power of Fun came from my first ever trip to the Phanatic's birthplace—the Galapagos Islands.

Shortly after I finished a mascot consulting and training gig in May 2009, for The College of William & Mary, I received a message from a young lady named Amy Cage. She introduced herself on the voice mail as a marketing representative from a travel company called Lindblad Expeditions. She wanted me to give her a ring back to discuss a potential Phillies-themed excursion to the Galapagos Islands.

Well, you don't receive messages like that every day and while I thought she had the wrong number—or at least should be contacting the Phillies directly—I called her right back. She told me she saw my name in a William & Mary alumni magazine article about me helping their mascot program and was surprised to learn I was the original Phillie Phanatic. She graduated from William & Mary and was now in New York working for Lindblad Expeditions. They were partners with the travel arm of National Geographic and her job was to develop themes for some of their excursions to destinations like Alaska, the Amazon and even the Galapagos Islands. She was looking into the possibility of organizing a sports theme for the next trip to explore the Galapagos when she saw my story. She did a little research on the Phanatic and discovered that he was actually from the Galapagos Islands! That's right, the Phanatic is from the Galapagos. It's a fact that only true Phanatic fans know. It's right there in the team's media guide.

The crazy story of the Phanatic's birth was hatched out of my frustration from being constantly asked who or what the Phanatic was shortly after he was introduced to Phillies fans in the spring of 1978.

"Are you an anteater?"

"Are you a bird?"

I don't know why these questions bugged me, but deep down inside I wanted to know who I was too!

We had a staff meeting about three weeks after the Phanatic's birth and in an exasperated tone, I explained that we needed to come up with an answer to the growing question of who and what the Phanatic was.

"He looks like a Darwin experiment gone wrong!" I said.

There was a pause and then someone responded, "That's it, he's from the Galapagos Islands!"

We quickly fashioned a simple back story for the Phanatic. His species was created when Darwin, while studying the Galapagos during a fateful experiment, made a miscalculation and unknowingly set in motion the creation of the Phanatics. This Phanatic species was so strange that even the creatures of the Galapagos didn't accept them. They were ridiculed and considered outcasts that didn't belong among the blue footed boobies, the albatrosses and the iguanas. When our Phanatic was born on the Islands, he grew to be one of the strongest and most independent of the entire clan, and while the Phanatics were still outcasts in their own homeland, our Phanatic was respected and admired by his own. Finally, the Phanatics decided they needed to find another place in this world where they would be accepted, so they challenged our Phanatic to go off and search for a new homeland for all of the Phanatics. He set off on a perilous journey around the world. It was difficult and fraught with many dangers, but after a few years on the sea, the Phanatic found the mouth of the Delaware and traveled north until he found the City of Brotherly Love. Veterans Stadium stood out to him because it reminded him of the strange rock formations on the shores of the Galapagos Islands. When he met the Phillies, they not only accepted him, they fell in love with him!

Happily, ever after!

Did I tell you I loved my job?

As Amy from Lindblad Expeditions acknowledged the Phanatic's back story, I realized she was calling with a legitimate request. I was impressed she took the time to research the Phanatic's heritage and the Phillies. She was asking for my help to make possible a Phillies expedition to the Galapagos. I explained to her that I no longer worked for the team—I left the club to start my own mascot consulting and entertainment business in 1999—that she'd have to take her request directly to the club and that I'd be happy to help with contacts. She was appreciative and we continued to talk about her job and how she had just finished developing a "Jeopardy!" cruise to the Galapagos that sold out, and Alex Trebek said it was the most amazing trip he had ever taken. This was one of the times when I regretted not being the Phanatic anymore. I was passing her off to the Phillies and wasn't going to be able to help make the trip a reality. She thanked me again and promised to let me know how it went when she contacted the Phillies. I was pretty sure the Phillies would be interested in the trip because they now took the Phanatic's back story very seriously. Tom Burgoyne had written a children's book for the Phillies called The *Phillie Phanatic's Galapagos Island Adventure.* In addition, the floor of the Phanatic's Attic, the retail store for all things Phanatic at Citizens Bank Park, had a map of the world printed on it with a hashtag line connecting the Galapagos Islands to Philadelphia.

The Phanatic is serious business and the Galapagos is where it all started.

A few weeks later, I got a call from Tom Burgoyne telling me the trip to the Galapagos was going to happen. He told me the club would send a small contingent of Phillies staff, a video crew, Tom and the Phanatic to capture footage for a new Phanatic video they were producing called *Time Travel Phanatic.* The Phanatic was going to travel back in time and witness his birth. So fun! So funny! And tangible proof of how important the Phanatic's story had become to the Phillies' marketing plan.

After a few minutes on the phone, Tom gave me the best news of all: The Phillies felt it was only right to include me on the trip if I wanted to be part of it.

Really?

Are you kidding me?

I was all in.

A few months later, on the day after Thanksgiving, I found myself on a plane to Ecuador, heading to the Galapagos Islands for the trip of a lifetime—and to my great glee, nature's validation of the Power of Fun.

We stayed overnight in the hotel Colon in Guayaquil, Ecuador. The next day, we boarded a plane to fly two hours west to the Galapagos Islands. I wrote a short blog post that morning about the history of Ecuador saying, "Ecuador's population is a bit over 13 million. The Inca Empire conquered this land in the 15th century." And then I quipped, "I saw both a McDonald's and a Hooters on the way to the airport." A true sign that the apocalypse was upon us!

I kept thinking what a wonderful opportunity this was for me, but I was very nervous because I was deathly afraid of being seasick, and we were, after all, going to be spending 10 days on the *National Geographic Endeavor,* a former exploration vessel turned into a luxury cruise ship. I tried my best to talk myself out of going because of that fear and also for concern about my business. I expressed my reservations to my wife Sandy and she played the Power of Fun card on me.

"Hey, Mr. Emperor of Fun," she said. "This will be an experience greater than any time lost at work. You need to take your own advice about the value of fun and go on the trip!"

My concern was, like many small-business owners today, I had to focus on the things in my life that seemed most important. You know, work, schedules, cell phones, iPads and to-do lists. I had received good business advice from very bright people since I decided to become my own boss and most of it was about focus: *Don't be distracted by bright shiny objects. Plan today for tomorrow, next week and the next quarter. Metrics, budgets and meetings about metrics. All for achieving small business success in this economy.* Distractions can be deadly. I feared the trip to the Galapagos, one of the most unique and fascinating places in the world, would become a distraction! What would happen if I disconnected from my business for a week and lost a little focus?

I found out very quickly. Those ten days on the *National Geographic Endeavor*, visiting places that I couldn't even dream about, made the "distraction" well worth it. But even better, it enhanced my business, because on that trip I found the greatest validation for the Power of Fun that I could ever have imagined—and it came from a very unexpected source.

There are many beautiful and strange creatures native to the Galapagos. The native sea lions really caught my eye. Though they look like any other sea lion, they are one-of-a-kind. And, to the delight of the Funsters on our trip, these sea lions, along with almost all of the animals and birds on the islands, have absolutely no fear of humans. We witnessed this phenomenon shortly after our plane landed. We shuttled by bus down to the harbor where the *Endeavor* was docked and waiting for us. We walked down to a cement dock to load on Zodiac rafts to take us to the ship. Right there, on the dock next to a couple of tourists, lay a sea lion. It was amazing. Not only was he not afraid of us, he actually looked bored! You could go right up to him and take pictures. Anything but touching. That was one of the strict rules we were taught right away by the naturalists and we would come to know it quite well over the next week. My job was to be the Phanatic's muscle during the trip. Translation: I was his spotter.

Our first mission was to get the Phanatic out on the shores of San Cristobal and capture as many pictures with sea lions and land iguanas as we could. We would disembark onto one of the Zodiac rafts with 150-horsepower engines. They reminded me of the old Navy Seal movies where the Navy Seals would roll over backward into the ocean in their flippers and masks. The Zodiac would take us right up to the shore and we would jump out and drag it onto the sand. They call it a wet landing and it made sense because we all got pretty wet! Tom Burgoyne and I had to hold the heavy Phanatic bag above our heads because the big, green guy would not have done well with a wet landing.

Our naturalist that day was named Celso Montalvo. He was born in Guayaquil, Ecuador, and at age 9 came to the Galapagos and never left. He was incredibly passionate about the Galapagos and made sure we appreciated what an extraordinary place it was—like no other on the planet! Celso is also a well-known environmentalist and advocate for the conservation of protected lands. Google him so you can have the pleasure of hearing directly from him. By the end of our trip, I had become close with Celso in part because of his passion for his work, but mostly because he was so interesting and fun to be around.

Celso escorted Tom and I to a small clearing inside a large outcrop of bushes and trees. It was just enough space for Tom to transform into the Phanatic, while I stood guard, ready to fend off any strange creatures that got too curious. Celso told us not to give any water to the mockingbirds because they would not leave us alone if we did. Sure enough, just minutes after we pulled the Phanatic costume out of the bag, a little mockingbird hopped right up on top of one of the Phanatic's shoes. I quickly snapped one of my favorite pictures of the trip. That little bird could not have cared less about us and with no fear pecked at the aluminum water canister that lay in the sand next to the shoes. What an amazing place, I thought. But it was just the start of things to come.

I want to share with you Celso's celebration of the Power of Fun with this anecdote:

The Phanatic, in all of his green glory, emerged from his "dressing room" among the bushes, with me, the spotter, tagging behind. Upon emerging, the Phanatic made a beeline toward a cute little sea lion pup that upon further review was probably more like a teenage sea lion. In a very high-pitched and excited voice, Celso exclaimed, "Oh, Phanatic, you have met your very first native friend from the Galapagos! What a wonderful moment for you."

Our cameras captured the moment and it was a sight to see: The Phanatic and the sea lion, like the long-lost relatives they were, waddling around together, posing for pictures. It was like a joyous family reunion. As the Phanatic and the sea lion frolicked, I noticed two adult sea lions about 100 yards in the distance. One of them perked up a bit and took notice of us mostly because of the commotion we were making and then, with a very loud grunt, dropped its head back down in the sand, rolled over and ignored us. I asked Celso if those sea lions were part of a group that included this little pup that the Phanatic was having an adventure with. He first complimented me for my observation (which I later learned was his way of making everyone around him feel smart) then told me the sea lion who grunted at us happened to be the mother of the Phanatic's playmate.

I was stunned to hear this.

"So why isn't the mother sea lion charging over here to protect her child?" I asked Celso. After all, I assumed, she surely had never seen anything like the Phanatic before. Wasn't she afraid that the unfamiliar green, furry guy would eat her young pup?

Celso looked at me with a smile that a father might have when trying to make his son understand something obvious.

"David," he said, "the Galapagos sea lions are endemic to the Galapagos. No other sea lions like these exist anywhere on the Earth. They have virtually no natural predators that can threaten them here and, over millions of years, they have selected out the gene for fear."

Celso's lesson continued.

"Not only that," he said, "but they have selected in the gene for play because they teach their young to fish through play. Galapagos sea lions usually die from starvation because adult sea lions will not feed older adults that are too old to fish."

I became really excited after Celso told me this because it was the best validation for my theory of the Power of Fun that I could ever hope to find. It had nothing to do with sports or the corporate world. No, even better, it was right from the theory of evolution!

I quickly explained to Celso my theory of the Power of Fun and told him I spoke to groups about using it to make them healthy and happier in their lives.

Celso's eyes widened and he became very excited.

"Well, David," he said, "you now have validation directly from Mother Nature because you can now tell your audiences that a species has not only survived—but thrived—by learning how to play!"

This is Synthesized Fun at its best—and from an unexpected source and place. Celso's willingness to share his passion for the beauty and wonder of the Galapagos Islands led to a fantastic and memorable validation of the Power of Fun.

If it works for the survival of one of the Galapagos Islands' greatest Funster species, it can work for you. It's like what George Bernard Shaw once said: "We don't stop playing because we grow old, we grow old because we stop playing!"

Synthesized Fun
"Oh, the new car smell!"

Working as the Phanatic for over 16 years afforded me a very unique perspective. Though I did not realize it at first, it was the Power of Fun that I learned from the Phanatic that helped me overcome a series of difficult challenges in my life. That perspective allowed me to "synthesize" fun into my consciousness. Synthesized Fun allows us to see Powerful Fun working, sometimes unexpectedly, in our lives. Like Michael Jack Schmidt winning over the Philly fans or the Galapagos sea lions thriving with play, the Power of Fun is a force working, at times unexpectedly, all around us.

Think about the last time you bought a new car. First, you looked for the best car that would fit your needs both on an emotional and practical level. Then you compared one car to another. You read and studied all of the standard and optional components of your favorite style and brand. You zeroed in on the car for you, haggled over price and purchased *your* brand-new car. You loved your choice and couldn't wait to start driving it and showing it off. Once on the road, however, you started to notice it seemed like everyone and their sister had bought the very same car! Those cars were always there when you were driving your old clunker, but now your new car had become synthesized in your consciousness and that caused you to see it everywhere. Expertise and proficiency are born out of the same type of synthesis.

Most experts, you could say, are synthesized in their fields. That is where I am with regard to the Power of Fun. My path wasn't planned by any means, but my experiences performing as the Phanatic gave me a very unique perspective and helped me develop a set of skills that I previously wasn't aware were even available. In the beginning of my career, I was just glad that I had a job. Very quickly, after the Phanatic was introduced, I understood the good fortune of working and getting paid to have fun. That was, after all, my first directive from Mr. Giles: "Just have fun." I also realized that my job was one many people would have killed for. That made me fear for my security. Anyone could do it—anyone could have fun, right?

When my job became a full-time position after that first summer and I received my first raise, the fear only grew. It was paralyzing at times. I would contemplate the very real possibility that a Phillies executive would eventually point out, "We're paying a lot of money for Mr. Raymond to be stupid! Can't we find someone else to do 'stupid' for less?" And how could I have argued with them?

For most of my career, fear made me work harder and do my best to be relevant and funny. It would be the only way to keep fooling them, I thought. It wasn't until long after I left the Phillies and became an entrepreneur, that I was able to reflect on the work. I finally did give myself some credit for building something very effective in the field of sports marketing. Maybe more importantly, I realized that I had stumbled onto something that was even more potent: Each time I put that costume on, I immersed myself in the Power of Fun. I think of the encounters I had with kids who were suffering the pain and fear of illness, where the Phanatic distracted them, put smiles on their faces and prompted them to say, "I love you, Phanatic."

The Phanatic successfully entertained at a funeral and in places where you would think he wouldn't belong, like a Catholic Church on a Sunday, the private chambers of the Supreme Court and during a General Electric polymer engineers' conference. These reflections, and countless other examples, started to have an effect on how I felt about my time with the Phillies. I thought more about how I was responding to my work developing my business than how I handled myself as a father and husband. I realized my job performing and entertaining as the Phanatic contained a built-in distraction of fun. I would not have survived the loss of my mother to cancer and the dissolution of my marriage without that distraction. This was an epiphany!

I was constantly asked to speak to various groups over the years, but I struggled coming up with a message beyond fun and interesting stories about being the Phanatic. I started talking about why I felt the Phanatic was successful, not only as a mascot for the Phillies, but as an icon and positive symbol for the city of Phila-delphia. Eventually, I found my message and the Power of Fun began to be synthesized in my consciousness. I started to see the effect of fun in my life and in those around me. It is easy to be an Emperor of Fun. I adopted it as my title because it was a consis-tent reminder about making a simple choice to make fun part of how you approach life at every level. Unknowingly, I was taught all of this by a true master of Powerful Fun. The Phanatic's person-ality was born out of this theory that lay somewhere inside of me and came out because Bill Giles knew he needed to distract Phillies fans from the inevitable losses that come in a long baseball season. What was created became even bigger than what was envisioned and the Phanatic started to use fun to distract people from the pain and discomfort they were suffering in their own lives. The power to distract with fun is inside all of us. We just have to make the simple choice to use it each and every day. We need to synthesize the fun and begin to see how it is available everywhere to help us overcome life and business challenges. Once you start to invest in the Theory of Powerful Fun, it pays off in dividends you didn't believe were possible, just as you wouldn't believe the Phanatic could save Mike Schmidt from a mob scene!

CHAPTER 7
The Power of F.U.N. Model

I have lived a blessed life mostly because I was afforded an opportunity to connect on an emotional level with the most passionate sports fans in the world! The conduit for that connection was the Phanatic's personality. What blossomed from that personality was a message I wasn't expecting. That message is what brought the Power of Fun alive and continues to live in the big green guy today. My hope is that you have an understanding what it is like to Be the Phanatic and how you can tap into the Power of Fun to be happier, healthier and more productive in your life at home and at work.

So, we have all of these great stories about fun and the Phanatic and my stories. But, now what do we do? Did you notice that throughout this book a main, common theme emerged? Yep, it was **F.U.N.** Fun is powerful.

In 1978, I didn't realize there was a process developing along the way to help lead to the success of the Phanatic, the Phillies and me as a performer and a person. It wasn't until long after that I looked back and realized it was as simple as **F.U.N.** And, these simple lessons, the **F.U.N.** of fun are what make up our Power of Fun Model.

Take this model away from this book. Practice it. Utilize it. Learn it. This is the model we teach companies and individuals to help them leverage fun as a powerful brand extension—like the Phillies have done for more than 40 years with the Phanatic.

This is the model we use to teach individuals how to work with the best times and overcome the hard times to better their personal lives, professional lives, and workplace environments.

If you can remember **F.U.N.** and **Distracting Fun**, you can remember how powerful that fun can be as a tool for both your personal and professional lives. It was these four simple lessons that for the past 40-plus years have taught me more than I could have ever known.

The F.U.N. of Fun Model

For review, remember the following;

F is for the Force of Fun. Remember, like a good Jedi, this force is all around you. All you have to do is recognize it, value it and engage it. Once you do that, fun becomes easy to engage and like my first day of being the Phanatic, you too will understand the Force of Fun!

U is for Universal. Fun can literally work anywhere. As the Phanatic, I was in churches, electrical engineer conferences, the private residences of the Kennedy family at Hickory Hill, at events all around the world, car dealerships, malls, corporations, company picnics and, yes, even a funeral. If fun works at a funeral then where will it not work? Fun is universal!

N is for "NO!" the Battle Cry of the Funkiller. Remember how important the voice of the Funkiller is to keep us safe and on course. Identify the Funkillers, embrace them and make them part of the creative team when the time is right and this "fun" will become twice as powerful!

Distracting Fun is important too. Remember, not all times are happy and filled with Phanatical-Phun. Embrace the challenges. Create simple mechanisms in your own life to identify those negative brain biases and moments that just seem to beat you down. Know that they can be overcome. Know they will come again. Use fun to distract you during the most difficult times in your life!

So, again, just remember **F.U.N.** and **Distracting Fun**. These principles are what we teach through interactive workshops and experiences and of course with this book. And, we truly hope they help you become happier, healthier and more productive at home and at work!

Chapter 8
The Phanatic's Top Five!

Yes, I learned a lot from the big green guy once I started to pay attention to what he was telling me. It took me almost 17 years to realize what the Phanatic was whispering in my ear during every interaction with a fan, every appearance, every ballgame or every hospital visit. The good news is you will learn all of that by Being the Phanatic, just like I did, and it will only take you a few hours by reading this book. You now know the four most important lessons that Being the Phanatic can teach you, but how can you use those to be happier right now? Well the big green guy wanted me to share with you his Top Five ways to be happier now and it won't cost you anything but your focus and energy.

1. A Moment to Pause

The personality I instilled in the Phanatic was a combination of slapstick comedy mixed with a dose of Daffy Duck and pinch of Philadelphia sports fan passion. He was and continues to be frenetic, hyper and constantly moving. As a performer, that was exhausting, but the fans related to it, so I kept it up as much as possible. When I needed a break, I would just have the Phanatic stop and stare at a random fan. This gave me the chance to catch my breath, but I quickly realized how entertaining it was for all the other fans. It was unusual for the Phanatic to be motionless, so it grabbed their attention and then the unlucky fan being stared at felt uncomfortable and always responded in some comical way, vocally or non-verbally. I remember one big leather-lunged guy who was the subject of this unexpected spotlight. He responded by yelling, "Hey, this ain't a f-ing Muppet Show!" Hysterical!

Similarly, our lives can be frenetic, hyper and exhausting at times. Deadlines, conflicts and obligations. To-do lists get longer and longer with no end in sight. Our Negative Brain Bias is in full effect during times of stress and it is so easy to lose perspective and get caught in a downward spiral of negativity. Sometimes we need a Moment to Pause so we can reboot. Here is what the Phanatic wants you to try and it only takes about 90 seconds or so.

A Moment to Pause is usually most effective first thing in the morning or just before bed. Get to a quiet place, close your eyes, take three deep breaths and then think of something that brings you great joy. This is personal so it can be anything that is joyful for you. My wife, Sandy, loved this when I asked her what she would think about. It immediately reminded her of how much she loved to smell our kids' hair after baths when they were infants. That smell of baby shampoo and the wonderful feeling of holding them close as they were all wrapped up in a warm blanket was what brought her pure joy.

Once you have taken those three breaths, relax and think of what brings you pure joy. Then, I want you to go there! Use all of your senses. Smell the aromas, taste the flavors, hear the sounds and feel the textures. After 90 seconds, take a few more deep breaths and open your eyes. Just like Being the Phanatic, you will be surprised by the results you get by just stopping and taking this moment to pause. It will refresh your perspective and after some practice it will be a go-to exercise that will make you happier now!

2. A Playlist For You

The Phanatic always connected emotionally to Philadelphia fans. That was a big part of his successful introduction in 1978. It is also the same reason Philadelphia fans were infected with Gritty-mania over 40 years later. Once you connect emotionally, that bond is very difficult to break.

I always used music to help the Phanatic connect to Phillies fans during routines and pantomimes. It was the perfect complementary tool to distract fans from bad play on the field or to celebrate the good. Music formed an emotional and shared connection between the Phillie Phanatic and Phillies fans. You too can use music to connect emotionally. Most importantly it can help to motivate and inspire you!

Try this. Build three playlists for the express purpose of putting you in the correct emotional space to prepare for your day. One list will be to relax and calm, the second will be to pump you up and the third to make you smile or laugh.

Each song and playlist will be customized by you and it doesn't matter if it is a golden oldie or opera. All that matters is that it connects to you on an emotional level. Once you design it that way, it will be effective. This is such a great tool because you can change it up easily and you will always have your own personal daily motivation right in your pocket!

3. Random Act of Kindness

The Phanatic's job, if you think about it, was to deliver Random Acts of Kindness. Just by showing up, the Phillie Phanatic, distracted with fun and delivered joy everywhere he went. Even New York fans enjoyed having the Phanatic engage them. Well, of course, they would first yell, "Get out of my way, you big, fat green thing! But before you do, get over here and take a picture with my kids!"

The Phanatic was a Random Act of Kindness delivery machine and it was the main reason the job was so much fun. People who receive RAKs appreciate the surprising fun, but the one who delivers the RAK gets twice the benefit! Trust me, on most days I would go home with a smile on my face.

Try performing a RAK at least once a week. It can be as simple as buying the person's cup of coffee in line behind you or just helping someone with a simple task. Take note of how the recipient responds. Usually it starts with a bit of protesting. "Oh, you don't have to do that." Or, "I'm OK." Or, "No need to bother." Once they see you insist, a big smile will come across their face and a pleasant conversation will start. That is always my favorite part because that conversation leads to an emotional connection you otherwise would have not created. Finally, I usually will add a request for them to pass the RAK along to someone else they come across later in the day. That way the RAKs will multiply. The person who delivers RAKs has the pleasure of anticipating the fun just before it is delivered, and on top of that gets to see the wonderful results. Twice the benefit in delivering the RAK than just receiving one!

After my Power of Fun presentations, I get the chance to meet and chat with a lot of the attendees. It is great fun and I love the feedback. RAKs seem to be a highlight of my talk because everyone wants to share their experiences with delivering them. One of my favorites was with a young lady from a large sports organization who had a talent for crafting. She put those skills to good use by painting small stones with bright colors and then carefully printing words of encouragement on them like "smile" or "love ." They were beautiful works of art and she would leave them in public places knowing someone would come along and find them. It was fun for her to try to imagine who would find them and how they might randomly brighten that person's day. After speaking with her and giving her my business card, I was surprised to receive a small package in the mail containing a personalized surprise just for me. It was one of her painted stones with the word FUN on it. It now sits on the mantle above my desk to remind me just how much Random Acts of Kindness make me happier!

4. Smile

Smiles are the Phillie Phanatic's currency. That is what he is in search of. Imagine being in front of thousands of smiling faces almost all the time. How would that make you feel? I can tell you that when I was inside that Phanatic costume, it was the best high you can imagine. Everyone calling your name, professing love for you, laughs and smiles for as far as I could see. Wow!

Smiles are probably the most powerful form of non-verbal communication. A smile feels warm and can disarm someone quickly even during stressful times and a smile can heal disappointment, as well. It is simple to do and takes almost no effort. Challenge yourself to smile as much as possible in one day. Smile at strangers with a nod of your head. Smile as you greet everyone you meet. Smile before you begin speaking and smile as you are listening. Smile when someone isn't smiling at you. As you do this notice how people respond to you and how it makes you feel to use a smile more than any other non-verbal cue. Celebrate your crow's feet as they are in part due to you using the Duchenne smile.

Named after Guillaume Duchenne, the psychiatrist who studied it, the Duchenne smile is one that uses all the muscles of your face and cannot be faked. It is genuine and powerful. Forget the Botox and leave those crow's feet in place. They are the Funster's Badge of Honor! Do your best to smile loud and proud as much as you possibly can because it will make those around you feel better, and if you practice this technique you will see your mood affected and driven toward happiness, too.

5. Be Grateful

The greatest job you could ever imagine was dropped in my lap in the summer of 1978. My prime directive was to have fun, get paid to watch the game I loved and watch my heroes who eventually became my friends. How could I not be grateful? It seemed to be an everyday part of the job. Looking back, Being the Phanatic infused me with the Power of Fun and being grateful was just another fringe benefit.

One of my favorite books is *The Happiness Equation* by Neil Pasricha. Neil points out, with regard to being grateful, we have all won the lottery each and every day when we wake up. Think of all those who are dead and gone. They can't take a breath, get up, walk and tell those around us how much we love them. Being grateful should be easy for us to do yet many of us don't take the time to do it.

Try to take account of what you are grateful for. Being alive is a great start, but after a while you will find so much more to be grateful for. It has been proven that those of us who regularly take time to remember how appreciative we are for the things we have are happier and healthier than those who don't.

Be grateful! Be happier!

Those are the Phillie Phanatic's Top Five ways to be happier now—no sweat, no smell, no muss. Peering through those big, googly eyes can help you focus on some pretty important emotional intelligence. So now what I want you to do is add your top five to the Phanatic's list and share them with your friends and let them know what Being the Phanatic is all about!

The Power of Fun for You
Final Thoughts

I want you to take my stories, take my experiences, and apply them in your daily personal and work lives. My hope is that you will have fun synthesized in your consciousness. You will see The Power of Fun working around you and, eventually through you. The Power of Fun will help during life struggles and will allow you to thrive when life is good. Just Be the Phanatic and remember that happiness is a skill set that can be attained through practice.

At The Power of Fun (daveraymondspeaks.com) and with my speaking, we offer on-going consultations, trainings, one-on-one coaching, live and virtual workshops—all focused on achievements to help you realize that fun can be powerful for you and those around you.

About the Author

Dave Raymond
The OG Phanatic/
Marketing Executive

Dave Raymond was the OG Phillie Phanatic in 1978. He retired from his mascot performance career in 1994 and started work with various companies including Capital One, every major sport league in the world, and countless colleges, universities and conferences to share The Power of Fun™ with them to create brand-ROI and professional development tools that matter.

To date, Dave's projects have generated billions of dollars in ROI of advertising and support for his clients and his work has been featured everywhere from *The Wall Street Journal*, CNN and ESPN to *The Tonight Show with Jimmy Fallon*.

Now, Dave speaks around the world about The Power of Fun™, sharing his model and on-going training on how to make work and personal life more meaningful and fulfilling.

Book him at **daveraymondspeaks.com**.